BIG JUST GOT BIGGER

Designs by Kim Hargreaves • Martin Storey
Carol Meldrum • Leah Sutton
Laura Long • Anna Wheeler

Above & right Blossom in Biggy Print,
right Doll in Big Wool both by Kim Hargreaves

4

Left Bisto in Big Wool by Martin Storey,
above Vinster in Big Wool by Carol Meldrum

Left Pia in Big Wool Tuft,
above Fifi in Chunky Print,
both by Kim Hargreaves

9

Left Coty, above Rilla
both in Chunky Print
& both by Kim Hargreaves

11

Left Nan in Chunky Print & Doll in Big Wool & Big Wool Tuft,
both by Kim Hargreaves, above Ovaltine in Biggy Print & Big Wool,
Oxo in Chunky Print, both by Martin Storey

Above Emma in Big Wool & Biggy Print,
right Hannah in Chunky & Biggy Print,
both by Laura Long

Left Beau in Biggy Print, above
Wanda in Chunky Print,
both by Kim Hargreaves

Left Pia in Biggy Print by Kim Hargreaves,
above Rene in Big Wool by Leah Sutton

Left Sis in Big Wool & Dixie in Chunky Print,
both by Kim Hargreaves, above Mingle & Click-Clack
in Big Wool, both by Anna Wheeler

Ovaltine in Biggy Print & Big Wool by Martin Storey,
Megan in Biggy Print by Laura Long

Roxie & Baxter both in Chunky Print
& Regan in Biggy Print, all by Kim Hargreaves

Above Floss in Chunky Print & Biggy Print by Kim Hargreaves,
right Virginia in Chunky Print & Big Wool Tuft by Leah Sutton

Left Foxy in Chunky Print & Big Wool
by Carol Meldrum, above Sis in Big Wool & Biddy
in Chunky Print, both by Kim Hargreaves

Left Fanny in Big Wool, above Ona in Big Wool and
Regan in Biggy Print, all by Kim Hargreaves

BIG JUST GOT BIGGER

Index

Baxter & Dixie both in Chunky Print
& both by Kim Hargreaves

No 1

HANNAH

LAURA LONG

YARN

	XS	S	M	L	XL	
To fit bust	81	86	91	97	102	cm
	32	34	36	38	40	in

Rowan Chunky Print and Biggy Print

A Chunky Temper 073
| | | 5 | 6 | 6 | 6 | 6 x 100gm |

B Biggy Humbug 254
| | | 8 | 9 | 9 | 10 | 10 x 100gm |

NEEDLES

1 pair 7mm (no 2) (US 10½) needles
1 pair 8mm (no 0) (US 11) needles

BUTTONS – 1 x 00335

TENSION

10 sts and 12 rows to 10 cm measured over patterned stocking stitch using 8mm (US 11) needles.

BACK

Cast on 52 (54: 58: 60: 64) sts using 7mm (US 10½) needles and yarn A.
Work in garter st for 2 rows, ending with a WS row.
Change to 8mm (US 11) needles.
Starting and ending rows as indicated, using the **fairisle** technique as described on the information page and repeating the 10 row patt repeat throughout, cont in patt from chart for body, which is worked entirely in st st beg with a K row, as folls:
Cont straight until back measures 20 cm, ending with a WS row.
Keeping patt correct, dec 1 st at each end of next and foll 12th row. 48 (50: 54: 56: 60) sts.
Work 11 rows, ending with a WS row.

Inc 1 st at each end of next and foll 8th row. 52 (54: 58: 60: 64) sts, taking inc sts into patt.
Work a further 13 rows, ending with a WS row. (Back should measure 50 cm.)

Shape raglan armholes

Keeping patt correct, cast off 4 sts at beg of next 2 rows. 44 (46: 50: 52: 56) sts.
Dec 1 st at each end of next 1 (3: 5: 5: 7) rows, then on every foll alt row until 16 (16: 16: 18: 18) sts rem.
Work 1 row, ending with a WS row. Cast off.

LEFT FRONT

Cast on 31 (32: 34: 35: 37) sts using 7mm (US 10½) needles and yarn A.
Work in garter st for 2 rows, ending with a WS row.

Change to 8mm (US 11) needles.
Starting and ending rows as indicated, cont in patt from chart for body as folls:
Cont straight until left front measures 20 cm, ending with a WS row.
Keeping patt correct, dec 1 st at beg of next and foll 12th row. 29 (30: 32: 33: 35) sts.
Work 7 rows, ending with a WS row.

Shape for collar

Keeping colours correct as set by chart, now start to work collar section in rev st st as folls:
Row 1 (RS): K to last 2 sts, P2.
Row 2: K2, P to end.
Row 3: K to last 3 sts, P3.
Row 4: K3, P to end.
Row 5: Inc in first st, K to last 3 sts, P3.
30 (31: 33: 34: 36) sts.

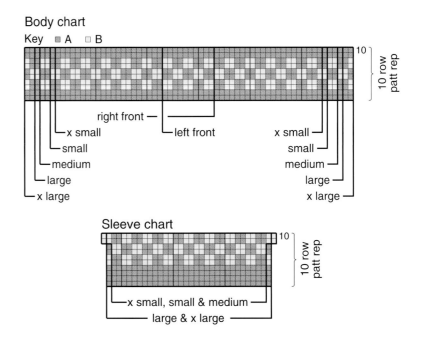

Body chart

Key ■ A □ B

right front — left front

x small — small — medium — large — x large

x small — small — medium — large — x large

10
10 row patt rep

Sleeve chart

x small, small & medium

large & x large

10
10 row patt rep

Row 6: As row 4.

Row 7: K to last 4 sts, P4.

Row 8: K4, P to end.

Rows 9 and 10: As rows 7 and 8.

Row 11: K to last 5 sts, P5.

Row 12: K5, P to end.

Row 13: Inc in first st, K to last 5 sts, P5. 31 (32: 34: 35: 37) sts.

Row 14: As row 12.

Working one extra st in rev st st on next and every foll 4th row as set by last 12 rows **throughout**, cont as folls:

Work a further 13 rows, ending with a WS row. (Left front should match back to beg of raglan armhole shaping.)

Shape raglan armhole

Keeping patt correct, cast off 4 sts at beg of next row. 27 (28: 30: 31: 33) sts.

Work 1 row.

Dec 1 st at raglan armhole edge of next 1 (3: 5: 5: 7) rows, then on every foll alt row until 17 (17: 17: 18: 18) sts rem.

Work 1 row, ending with a WS row.

Shape neck

Next row (RS): K2tog, patt 7 sts, wrap next st (by slipping next st onto right needle, taking yarn to opposite side of work between needles and then slipping same st back onto left needle – when working across sts, work the st and the wrapped loop as one st) and turn.

Next row: Patt 8 sts.

Next row: K2tog, patt 1 st, wrap next st and turn.

Next row: Patt 2 sts.

Break yarn and leave sts on a holder.

RIGHT FRONT

Cast on 31 (32: 34: 35: 37) sts using 7mm (US 10½) needles and yarn A.

Work in garter st for 2 rows, ending with a WS row.

Change to 8mm (US 11) needles.

Starting and ending rows as indicated, cont in patt from chart for body as folls:

Cont straight until right front measures 20 cm, ending with a WS row.

Keeping patt correct, dec 1 st at end of next and foll 12th row. 29 (30: 32: 33: 35) sts.

Work 5 rows, ending with a WS row.

Next row (buttonhole row) (RS): Patt 3 sts, cast off 2 sts, patt to end.

Next row: Patt to end, casting on 2 sts over those cast off on previous row.

Shape for collar

Keeping colours correct as set by chart, now start to work collar section in rev st st as folls:

Row 1 (RS): P2, K to end.

Row 2: P to last 2 sts, K2.

Row 3: P3, K to end.

Row 4: P to last 3 sts, K3.

Row 5: P3, K to last st, inc in last st. 30 (31: 33: 34: 36) sts.

Row 6: As row 4.

Row 7: P4, K to end.

Row 8: P to last 4 sts, K4.

Rows 9 and 10: As rows 7 and 8.

Row 11: P5, K to end.

Row 12: P to last 5 sts, K5.

Row 13: P5, K to last st, inc in last st. 31 (32: 34: 35: 37) sts.

Row 14: As row 12.

Working one extra st in rev st st on next and every foll 4th row as set by last 12 rows **throughout**, cont as folls:

Work a further 14 rows, ending with a RS row. (Right front should match back to beg of raglan armhole shaping.)

Shape raglan armhole

Keeping patt correct, cast off 4 sts at beg of next row. 27 (28: 30: 31: 33) sts.

Dec 1 st at raglan armhole edge of next 1 (3: 5: 5: 7) rows, then on every foll alt row until 16 (16: 16: 17: 17) sts rem, ending with a RS row.

Shape neck

Next row (WS): Patt 8 sts, wrap next st (by slipping next st onto right needle, taking yarn to opposite side of work between needles and then slipping same st back onto left needle – when working across sts, work the st and the wrapped loop as one st) and turn.

Next row: Patt to last 2 sts, K2tog.

Next row: Patt 2 sts, wrap next st and turn.

Do **NOT** break yarn and leave sts on a holder. (This ball of yarn will be used for collar.)

SLEEVES

Cast on 30 (30: 30: 32: 32) sts using 7mm (US 10½) needles and yarn A.

Work in garter st for 2 rows, ending with a WS row.

Change to 8mm (US 11) needles.

Starting and ending rows as indicated, cont in patt from chart for sleeves as folls:

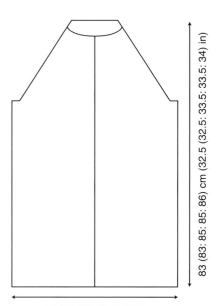

83 (83: 85: 85: 86) cm (32.5 (32.5: 33.5: 33.5: 34) in)

52 (54: 58: 60: 64) cm (20.5 (21.5: 23: 23.5: 25) in)

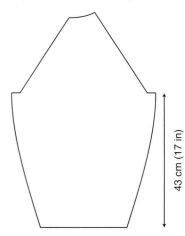

43 cm (17 in)

Inc 1 st at each end of 9th and every foll 12th (12th: 8th: 12th: 8th) row to 38 (38: 36: 40: 38) sts, then on every foll – (–: 10th: –: 10th) row until there are – (–: 40: –: 42) sts, taking inc sts into patt.

Cont straight until sleeve measures approx 43 cm, ending after same WS patt row as on back to beg of raglan armhole shaping.

Shape raglan

Keeping patt correct, cast off 4 sts at beg of next 2 rows. 30 (30: 32: 32: 34) sts.

Dec 1 st at each end of next and every foll 4th row to 24 (24: 26: 26: 28) sts, then on every foll alt row until 10 sts rem.

Work 1 row, ending with a WS row.

Left sleeve only

Dec 1 st at each end of next row, then cast off 2 sts at beg of foll row. 6 sts.

Dec 1 st at beg of next row, then cast off 3 sts at beg of foll row.

Right sleeve only

Cast off 3 sts at beg and dec 1 st at end of next row. 6 sts.

Work 1 row.

Rep last 2 rows once more.

Both sleeves

Cast off rem 2 sts.

MAKING UP

PRESS as described on the information page. Join raglan seams using back stitch, or mattress stitch if preferred.

Collar

With RS facing, using 7mm (US 10½) needles and ball of yarn left with right front, patt across 15 (15: 15: 16: 16) sts from right front holder, pick up and knit 6 sts from top of right sleeve, 16 (16: 16: 18: 18) sts from back, and 6 sts from top of left sleeve, then patt across 15 (15: 15: 16: 16) sts from left front holder. 58 (58: 58: 62: 62) sts.

Keeping patt correct as set by front sts, work in patt for 15 cm, ending with a P row.

Break off yarn B and cont using yarn A only.

Next row: Knit.

Cast off knitwise.

Front bands (both alike)

With RS facing, using 7mm (US 10½) needles and yarn A, pick up and knit 37 sts along front opening edge, between cast-on edge and start of collar shaping.

Cast off knitwise (on WS).

Collar bands (both alike)

With RS of collar section (WS of body) facing, using 7mm (US 10½) needles and yarn A, pick up and knit 55 (55: 57: 57: 59) sts along front opening edge of collar section, between cast-off edge and start of collar shaping.

Cast off knitwise (on WS).

See information page for finishing instructions.

No 2

REGAN

KIM HARGREAVES

YARN

Rowan Biggy Print

5 x 100gm

(photographed in Giddy 239 and Slippery 235)

NEEDLES

1 pair 20mm (US 36) needles

TENSION

5½ sts and 8 rows to 10 cm measured over moss stitch using 20mm (US 36) needles.

FINISHED SIZE

Completed scarf measures 20 cm (8 in) wide and 230 cm (90½ in) long (excluding fringe).

SCARF

Cast on 11 sts using 20mm (US 36) needles.

Row 1 (RS): K1, (P1, K1) 5 times.

Row 2: As row 1.

These 2 rows form moss st.

Cont in moss st until scarf measures 230 cm, ending with a WS row.

Cast off in moss st.

MAKING UP

PRESS as described on the information page. Cut 30 cm lengths of yarn and knot groups of 3 of these lengths through ends of scarf, making 5 knots evenly spaced across each end.

YARN

	XS	S	M	L	XL	
To fit bust	81	86	91	97	102	cm
	32	34	36	38	40	in

Rowan Big Wool

Sweater 7 7 7 8 8 x 100gm
(photographed in Rascal 032)

Jacket 6 6 7 7 7 x 100gm
(photographed in Pip 015)

NEEDLES

1 pair 10mm (no 000) (US 15) needles
1 pair 12mm (US 17) needles
Jacket only: 9mm (no 00) crochet hook

RIBBON – **Jacket only**: 130 cm of 2.5 cm
wide ribbon

TENSION

8 sts and 12 rows to 10 cm measured over
stocking stitch using 12mm (US 17) needles.

Sweater

BACK

Lower section

Cast on 36 (38: 40: 42: 44) sts using 12mm
(US 17) needles.
Row 1 (RS): K1 (0: 0: 0: 1), P2 (0: 1: 2: 2),
(K2, P2) 0 (1: 1: 1: 1) times, (K2, P3) twice,
(K2, P2) twice, (K2, P3) twice, K2, (P2, K2) 0
(1: 1: 1: 1) times, P2 (0: 1: 2: 2), K1 (0: 0: 0: 1).
Row 2: P1 (0: 0: 0: 1), K2 (0: 1: 2: 2), (P2, K2)
0 (1: 1: 1: 1) times, (P2, K3) twice, (P2, K2)
twice, (P2, K3) twice, P2, (K2, P2) 0 (1: 1: 1:
1) times, K2 (0: 1: 2: 2), P1 (0: 0: 0: 1).
These 2 rows form rib.
Cont in rib for a further 14 rows, ending with
a WS row.

Row 17 (RS): Work 2 tog, rib 4 (5: 6: 7: 8),
P2tog, K2, P2tog tbl, rib 12, P2tog, K2,
P2tog tbl, rib to last 2 sts, work 2 tog.
30 (32: 34: 36: 38) sts.
Cont in rib until lower section measures 22 cm,
ending with a WS row.
Cast off in rib.

Upper section

With **WS** facing (so that ridge is formed on
RS of work) and using 12mm (US 17) needles,
pick up and knit 30 (32: 34: 36: 38) sts along
cast-off edge of lower section.
Beg with a K row, work in st st for 4 rows.
Next row (RS): K2, M1, K to last 2 sts, M1, K2.
Working all increases as set by last row, inc 1 st
at each end of every foll 6th row until there
are 36 (38: 40: 42: 44) sts.
Cont straight until back measures 40 (41: 41:
42: 42) cm from cast-on edge of lower
section, ending with a WS row.

Shape armholes

Cast off 2 sts at beg of next 2 rows.
32 (34: 36: 38: 40) sts.
Dec 1 st at each end of next 2 (2: 3: 3: 4) rows,
then on foll alt row. 26 (28: 28: 30: 30) sts.
Cont straight until armhole measures 20 (20:
21: 21: 22) cm, ending with a WS row.

Shape shoulders and back neck

Next row (RS): Cast off 3 sts, K until there
are 5 (6: 6: 6: 6) sts on right needle and turn,
leaving rem sts on a holder.
Work each side of neck separately.
Cast off 2 sts at beg of next row.
Cast off rem 3 (4: 4: 4: 4) sts.
With RS facing, rejoin yarn to rem sts, cast off
centre 10 (10: 10: 12: 12) sts, K to end.
Complete to match first side, reversing
shapings.

FRONT

Work as given for back until 8 (8: 8: 10: 10) rows
less have been worked than on back to start of
shoulder shaping, ending with a WS row.

Shape neck

Next row (RS): K10 (11: 11: 12: 12) and
turn, leaving rem sts on a holder.
Work each side of neck separately.
Dec 1 st at neck edge of next 3 rows, then on
foll 1 (1: 1: 2: 2) alt rows. 6 (7: 7: 7: 7) sts.
Work 2 rows, ending with a WS row

Shape shoulder

Cast off 3 sts at beg of next row.
Work 1 row.
Cast off rem 3 (4: 4: 4: 4) sts.
With RS facing, rejoin yarn to rem sts, cast off
centre 6 sts, K to end.
Complete to match first side, reversing
shapings.

SLEEVES (both alike)

Lower section

Cast on 28 (28: 30: 30: 32) sts using 12mm
(US 17) needles.
Row 1 (RS): P1 (1: 2: 2: 1), ★K2, P2, rep
from ★ to last 3 (3: 4: 4: 3) sts, K2, P1 (1: 2: 2:
1).
Row 2: K1 (1: 2: 2: 1), ★P2, K2, rep from ★ to
last 3 (3: 4: 4: 3) sts, P2, K1 (1: 2: 2: 1).
These 2 rows form rib.
Cont in rib until lower section measures 22
cm, ending with a WS row.
Cast off in rib.

Upper section

With **WS** facing (so that ridge is formed on
RS of work) and using 12mm (US 17) needles,
pick up and knit 28 (28: 30: 30: 32) sts along
cast-off edge of lower section.

Beg with a K row, work in st st until sleeve measures 43 (43: 44: 44: 44) cm from cast-on edge of lower section, ending with a WS row.

Shape top

Cast off 2 sts at beg of next 2 rows.
24 (24: 26: 26: 28) sts.
Dec 1 st at each end of next and foll alt row, then on foll 4th row.
18 (18: 20: 20: 22) sts.
Work 1 row, ending with a WS row.
Dec 1 st at each end of next and every foll alt row to 14 sts, then on foll 3 rows, ending with a WS row.
Cast off rem 8 sts.

MAKING UP

PRESS as described on the information page.
Join right shoulder seam using back stitch, or mattress stitch if preferred.

Neckband

With RS facing and using 10mm (US 15) needles, pick up and knit 11 (11: 11: 12: 12) sts down left side of neck, 6 sts from front, 11 (11: 11: 12: 12) sts up right side of neck, then 14 (14: 14: 16: 16) sts from back.
42 (42: 42: 46: 46) sts.
Row 1 (WS): P2, ★K2, P2, rep from ★ to end.
Row 2: K2, ★P2, K2, rep from ★ to end.
Rep last 2 rows for 8 cm.
Cast off in rib.
See information page for finishing instructions, setting in sleeves using the set-in method.

Jacket

CROCHET ABBREVIATIONS

ch = chain; **ss** = slip stitch;
dc = double crochet; **ttr** = triple treble;
sp(s) = space(s).

LOWER SECTION (worked downwards in one piece)

Make 64 (68: 72: 76: 80) ch using 9.00mm crochet hook.
Row 1 (WS): 1 dc into 2nd ch from hook, 1 dc into each ch to end, turn.
63 (67: 71: 75: 79) sts.

Counting in from both ends of last row and placing markers on foundation ch edge, place markers after 17th (18th: 19th: 20th: 21st) st in from both ends of row, leaving 29 (31: 33: 35: 37) sts between markers. (These markers correspond with side seams of upper sections.)

Row 2: 1 ch (does NOT count as st), 1 dc into first dc, (6 ch, miss 3 dc, 1 dc into next dc) 2 (2: 2: 3: 2) times, (6 ch, miss 2 dc, 1 dc into next dc) 7 (5: 7: 5: 7) times, (6 ch, miss 3 dc, 1 dc into next dc) 1 (5: 3: 5: 5) times, (6 ch, miss 2 dc, 1 dc into next dc) 7 (5: 7: 5: 7) times, (6 ch, miss 3 dc, 1 dc into next dc) 2 (2: 2: 3: 2) times, turn.
19 (19: 21: 21: 23) ch sps.

Row 3: 8 ch (counts as 1 ttr and 3 ch), 1 dc into first ch sp, ★6 ch, 1 dc into next ch sp, rep from ★ to end, 3 ch, 1 ttr into dc at beg of previous row, turn.

Row 4: 1 ch (does NOT count as st), 1 dc into ttr at end of previous row, 6 ch, miss (3 ch and 1 dc), 1 dc into next ch sp, ★6 ch, 1 dc into next ch sp, rep from ★ to end, working dc at end of last rep into 5th of 8 ch at beg of previous row, turn.

Row 5: As row 3.

Row 6: 1 ch (does NOT count as st), 1 dc into ttr at end of previous row, 3 ch, miss (3 ch and 1 dc), 1 dc into next ch sp, ★3 ch, 1 dc into next ch sp, rep from ★ to end, working dc at end of last rep into 5th of 8 ch at beg of previous row, turn.

Row 7: 1 ch (does NOT count as st), 2 dc into first ch sp, ★1 dc into next dc, 9 ch, miss 3 ch, 1 dc into next dc★★, 3 dc into next ch sp, rep from ★ to end, ending last rep at ★★, 2 dc into last ch sp, turn.

Row 8: 1 ch (does NOT count as st), 1 dc into each of first 2 dc, ★5 ch, miss 1 dc, 1 dc into next ch sp, 5 ch, miss 1 dc★★, 1 dc into each of next 3 dc, rep from ★ to end, ending last rep at ★★, 1 dc into each of last 2 dc, turn.

Row 9: 1 ch (does NOT count as st), 1 dc into first dc, ★5 ch, miss 1 dc, 1 dc into next dc, 5 ch, miss 1 dc, 1 dc into next dc, rep from ★ to end, turn.

Row 10: 1 ch (does NOT count as st), 1 dc into first dc, ★5 ch, (1 ss, 7 ch, 1 ss, 7 ch, 1 ss, 7 ch and 1 ss) into next dc, 5 ch, 1 dc into next dc, rep from ★ to end.
Fasten off.

BACK UPPER SECTION

With **WS** facing (so that ridge is formed on RS of work) and using 12mm (US 17) needles, pick up and knit 30 (32: 34: 36: 38) sts along foundation ch edge of lower section between markers.
Beg with a K row, work in st st for 4 rows.
Next row (RS): K2, M1, K to last 2 sts, M1, K2.
Working all increases as set by last row, inc 1 st at each end of 8th and foll 6th (8th: 8th: 8th: 8th) row. 36 (38: 40: 42: 44) sts.
Work 3 (3: 3: 5: 5) rows, ending with a WS row. (Back should measure 19 (20: 20: 21: 21) cm from pick-up row.)

Shape armholes

Cast off 2 sts at beg of next 2 rows.
32 (34: 36: 38: 40) sts.
Dec 1 st at each end of next 2 (2: 3: 3: 4) rows, then on foll alt row. 26 (28: 28: 30: 30) sts.
Cont straight until armhole measures 20 (20: 21: 21: 22) cm, ending with a WS row.

Shape shoulders

Cast off 3 (4: 4: 4: 4) sts at beg of next 2 rows, then 4 sts at beg of foll 2 rows.
Cast off rem 12 (12: 12: 14: 14) sts.

LEFT FRONT UPPER SECTION

With **WS** facing (so that ridge is formed on RS of work) and using 12mm (US 17) needles, pick up and knit 17 (18: 19: 20: 21) sts along foundation ch edge of lower section between front opening edge and left side seam marker.
Beg with a K row, work in st st for 4 rows.
Next row (RS): K2, M1, K to end.
18 (19: 20: 21: 22) sts.
Working all side seam increases as set by last row, cont as folls:
Work 5 rows.
Next row (RS): K to last 7 sts, sl 1, K2tog, psso, K4. 16 (17: 18: 19: 20) sts.

Working all front slope decreases as set by last row, cont as folls:

Inc 1 st at side seam edge on 2nd and foll 6th (8th: 8th: 8th: 8th) row **and at same time** dec 0 (2: 2: 2: 2) sts at front slope edge on 0 (10th: 10th: 8th: 10th) row.
18 (17: 18: 19: 20) sts.

Work 3 (3: 3: 5: 5) rows, dec 2 (0: 0: 0: 0) sts at front slope edge on 2nd (0: 0: 0: 0) row and ending with a WS row. 16 (17: 18: 19: 20) sts.

Shape armhole

Cast off 2 sts at beg and dec 0 (0: 0: 2: 0) sts at front slope edge of next row.
14 (15: 16: 15: 18) sts.

Work 1 row.

Dec 1 st at armhole edge of next 2 (2: 3: 3: 4) rows, then on foll alt row **and at same time** dec 0 (0: 2: 0: 2) sts at front slope edge on 0 (0: 5th: 0: next) row. 11 (12: 10: 11: 11) sts.

Dec 2 sts at front slope edge **only** on 3rd (next: 10th: 2nd: 3rd) and foll 8th (10th: 0: 0: 0) row. 7 (8: 8: 9: 9) sts.

L and XL sizes only

Work 7 rows, ending with a WS row.

Next row (RS): K1, K2tog tbl, K6. 8 sts.

All sizes

Cont straight until left front matches back to start of shoulder shaping, ending with a WS row.

Shape shoulder

Cast off 3 (4: 4: 4: 4) sts at beg of next row.

Work 1 row.

Cast off rem 4 sts.

RIGHT FRONT UPPER SECTION

With **WS** facing (so that ridge is formed on RS of work) and using 12mm (US 17) needles, pick up and knit 17 (18: 19: 20: 21) sts along foundation ch edge of lower section between right side seam marker and front opening edge.

Beg with a K row, work in st st for 4 rows.

Next row (RS): K to last 2 sts, M1, K2.
18 (19: 20: 21: 22) sts.

Working all side seam increases as set by last row, cont as folls:

Work 5 rows.

Next row (RS): K4, sl 1, K1, psso, slip st now on right needle back onto left needle and lift 2nd st on left needle over this st and off left needle, then slip same st back onto right needle (2 sts decreased), K to end.
16 (17: 18: 19: 20) sts.

Working all front slope decreases as set by last row, complete to match left front, reversing shapings.

SLEEVES (both alike)

Lower section (worked downwards)

Make 26 ch using 9.00mm crochet hook.

Row 1 (RS): 1 dc into 2nd ch from hook, 1 dc into each ch to end, turn. 25 sts.

Row 2: 1 ch (does NOT count as st), 1 dc into each of first 3 dc, (9 ch, miss 3 dc, 1 dc into each of next 5 dc) twice, 9 ch, miss 3 dc, 1 dc into each of last 3 dc, turn.

Now work rows 8 to 10 as given for lower section.

Fasten off.

Upper section

With **WS** facing (so that ridge is formed on RS of work) and using 12mm (US 17) needles, pick up and knit 24 (24: 26: 26: 26) sts along foundation ch edge of lower section.

Beg with a K row and working all increases in same way as for side seam increases, cont in st st, shaping sides by inc 1 st at each end of 17th (17th: 17th: 17th: 13th) and every foll 16th (16th: 16th: 16th: 10th) row until there are 28 (28: 30: 30: 32) sts.

Cont straight until sleeve measures 37 (37: 38: 38: 38) cm from pick-up row, ending with a WS row.

Shape top

Cast off 2 sts at beg of next 2 rows.
24 (24: 26: 26: 28) sts.

Dec 1 st at each end of next and foll alt row, then on foll 4th row.
18 (18: 20: 20: 22) sts.

Work 1 row, ending with a WS row.

Dec 1 st at each end of next and every foll alt row to 14 sts, then on foll 3 rows, ending with a WS row.

Cast off rem 8 sts.

MAKING UP

PRESS as described on the information page. Join both shoulder seams using back stitch, or mattress stitch if preferred.

Edging

With RS facing and using 9.00mm crochet hook, work a row of dc evenly along entire front opening and neck edges.

Fasten off.

See information page for finishing instructions, setting in sleeves using the set-in method. Cut ribbon into 2 equal lengths and attach to inside of front opening edges level with pick-up row.

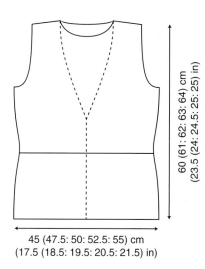

60 (61: 62: 63: 64) cm
(23.5 (24: 24.5: 25: 25) in)

45 (47.5: 50: 52.5: 55) cm
(17.5 (18.5: 19.5: 20.5: 21.5) in)

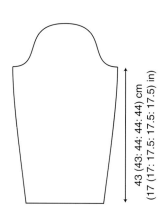

43 (43: 44: 44: 44) cm
(17 (17: 17.5: 17.5: 17.5) in)

Oxo

MARTIN STOREY

YARN

	S	M	L	XL	XXL	
To fit chest	97	102	107	112	117	cm
	38	40	42	44	46	in

Rowan Chunky Print

| | 12 | 13 | 13 | 14 | 15 | x 100gm |

(photographed in Temper 073)

NEEDLES

1 pair 7mm (no 2) (US 10½) needles
1 pair 8mm (no 0) (US 11) needles
Cable needle

TENSION

18 sts and 17 rows to 10 cm measured over
cable pattern using 8mm (US 11) needles.

SPECIAL ABBREVIATIONS

C10B = slip next 5 sts onto cable needle and
leave at back of work, K5, then K5 from cable
needle.
C10F = slip next 5 sts onto cable needle and
leave at front of work, K5, then K5 from cable
needle.

BACK

Cast on 63 (65: 69: 71: 73) sts using 7mm
(US 10½) needles.
Row 1 (RS): K0 (0: 0: 1: 2), P0 (1: 3: 3: 3),
★K3, P3, rep from ★ to last 3 (4: 0: 1: 2) sts,
K3 (3: 0: 1: 2), P0 (1: 0: 0: 0).
Row 2: P0 (0: 0: 1: 2), K0 (1: 3: 3: 3), ★P3, K3,
rep from ★ to last 3 (4: 0: 1: 2) sts, P3 (3: 0: 1: 2),
K0 (1: 0: 0: 0).
These 2 rows form rib.
Cont in rib for a further 7 rows, ending with
a RS row.
Row 10 (WS): Rib 1 (1: 3: 2: 2), ★(rib 1, M1)

twice, rib 1, rep from ★ to last 2 (1: 3: 3: 2) sts,
rib to end. 103 (107: 111: 115: 119) sts.
Change to 8mm (US 11) needles.
Row 1 (RS): Knit.
Row 2 and every foll alt row: Purl.
Row 3: K14 (1: 3: 5: 7), ★C10F, K5, rep from
★ to last 14 (1: 3: 5: 7) sts, (C10F) 1 (0: 0: 0: 0)
times, K4 (1: 3: 5: 7).
Rows 5 and 7: Knit.
Row 9: K4 (1: 3: 5: 7), (C10B) 1 (0: 0: 0: 0)
times, ★K5, C10B, rep from ★ to last 14 (1: 3:
5: 7) sts, K14 (1: 3: 5: 7).
Row 11: Knit.
Row 12: Purl.
These 12 rows form patt.
Cont in patt until back measures 43 cm,
ending with a WS row.
Shape armholes
Keeping patt correct, cast off 6 sts at beg of
next 2 rows.
91 (95: 99: 103: 107) sts.
Dec 1 st at each end of next 5 rows, then on
foll 1 (2: 3: 4: 5) alt rows, then on foll 4th row.
77 (79: 81: 83: 85) sts.
Cont straight until armhole measures 23 (24:
25: 26: 27) cm, ending with a WS row.
Shape shoulders and back neck
Next row (RS): Cast off 12 sts, patt until
there are 15 (15: 16: 16: 16) sts on right
needle and turn, leaving rem sts on a holder.
Work each side of neck separately.
Cast off 3 sts at beg of next row.
Cast off rem 12 (12: 13: 13: 13) sts.
With RS facing, rejoin yarn to rem sts, cast off
centre 23 (25: 25: 27: 29) sts dec 10 sts evenly,
patt to end.
Complete to match first side, reversing
shapings.

FRONT

Work as given for back until 10 (10: 12: 12: 12)
rows less have been worked than on back to
start of shoulder shaping, ending with a WS row.
Shape neck
Next row (RS): Patt 30 (30: 32: 32: 32) sts
and turn, leaving rem sts on a holder.
Work each side of neck separately.
Dec 1 st at neck edge of next 3 rows, then on
foll 3 (3: 4: 4: 4) alt rows, ending with a WS row.
24 (24: 25: 25: 25) sts.
Shape shoulder
Cast off 12 sts at beg of next row.
Work 1 row.
Cast off rem 12 (12: 13: 13: 13) sts.
With RS facing, rejoin yarn to rem sts, cast off
centre 17 (19: 17: 19: 21) sts dec 8 sts evenly,
patt to end.
Complete to match first side, reversing
shapings.

SLEEVES (both alike)

Cast on 29 (29: 31: 33: 33) sts using 7mm
(US 10½) needles.
Row 1 (RS): P1 (1: 2: 3: 3), K3, ★P3, K3, rep
from ★ to last 1 (1: 2: 3: 3) sts, P1 (1: 2: 3: 3).
Row 2: K1 (1: 2: 3: 3), P3, ★K3, P3, rep from
★ to last 1 (1: 2: 3: 3) sts, K1 (1: 2: 3: 3).
These 2 rows form rib.
Cont in rib for a further 7 rows, ending with
a RS row.
Row 10 (WS): Rib 1 (1: 2: 3: 3), ★(rib 1,
M1) twice, rib 1, rep from ★ to last 1 (1: 2: 3:
3) sts, rib to end. 47 (47: 49: 51: 51) sts.
Change to 8mm (US 11) needles.
Row 1 (RS): Inc in first st, K to last st, inc in
last st. 49 (49: 51: 53: 53) sts.
Row 2 and every foll alt row: Purl.

Row 3: K2 (2: 3: 4: 4), *C10F, K5, rep from *
to last 2 (2: 3: 4: 4) sts, K2 (2: 3: 4: 4).
Row 5: As row 1. 51 (51: 53: 55: 55) sts.
Row 7: Knit.
Row 9: Inc in first st, K2 (2: 3: 4: 4), *K5,
C10B, rep from * to last 3 (3: 4: 5: 5) sts, K2
(2: 3: 4: 4), inc in last st. 53 (53: 55: 57: 57) sts.
Row 11: Knit.
Row 12: Purl.
These 12 rows form patt and start sleeve
shaping.
Cont in patt, shaping sides by inc 1 st at each
end of next and every foll 4th row to 61 (65:
67: 67: 73) sts, then on every foll 6th row until
there are 73 (75: 77: 79: 81) sts, taking inc sts
into patt.

Cont straight until sleeve measures 46 (47: 47:
48: 48) cm, ending with a WS row.
Shape top
Keeping patt correct, cast off 6 sts at beg of
next 2 rows.
61 (63: 65: 67: 69) sts.
Dec 1 st at each end of next 5 rows, then on
every foll alt row to 39 sts, then on foll 5 rows,
ending with a WS row. 29 sts.
Cast off 5 sts at beg of next 2 rows.
Cast off rem 19 sts, dec 9 sts evenly.

MAKING UP

PRESS as described on the information page.
Join right shoulder seam using back stitch, or
mattress stitch if preferred.

Collar
With RS facing and using 7mm (US 10½)
needles, pick up and knit 11 (12: 13: 14: 15) sts
down left side of neck, 8 (10: 8: 10: 12) sts
from front, 11 (12: 13: 14: 15) sts up right side
of neck, then 18 (20: 20: 22: 24) sts from back.
48 (54: 54: 60: 66) sts.
Row 1 (WS): *K3, P3, rep from * to end.
This row forms rib.
Cont in rib until collar measures 9 cm.
Change to 8mm (US 11) needles.
Cont in rib until collar measures 18 cm.
Cast off in rib.
See information page for finishing instructions,
setting in sleeves using the set-in method and
reversing collar seam for turn-back.

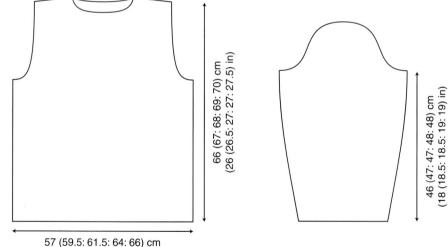

66 (67: 68: 69: 70) cm
(26 (26.5: 27: 27: 27.5) in)

57 (59.5: 61.5: 64: 66) cm
(22.5 (23.5: 24: 25: 26) in)

46 (47: 47: 48: 48) cm
(18 (18.5: 18.5: 19: 19) in)

No 5

NAN

KIM HARGREAVES

YARN

	XS	S	M	L	XL	
To fit bust	81	86	91	97	102	cm
	32	34	36	38	40	in

Rowan Chunky Print

6　6　6　7　7 x 100gm

(photographed in Native 072)

NEEDLES

1 pair 7mm (no 2) (US 10½) needles

1 pair 10mm (no 000) (US 15) needles

1 pair 12mm (US 17) needles

TENSION

12 sts and 13 rows to 10 cm measured over pattern using 12mm (US 17) needles.

SPECIAL ABBREVIATIONS

Cluster 2 = take yarn to back (RS) of work, slip 2 sts purlwise, bring yarn to front (WS) of work between needles and slip same 2 sts back onto left needle, take yarn to back (RS) of work, slip same 2 sts purlwise again and bring yarn to front (WS) of work between needles, thereby wrapping 2 sts to form cluster.

Pattern note: As row end edges form actual finished front opening edges of garment, it is important these edges are kept neat. Therefore avoid joining in new balls of yarn at these edges.

BACK

Cast on 52 (54: 58: 60: 64) sts using 10mm (US 15) needles.

Row 1 (RS): K0 (1: 1: 0: 0), *K2tog, (yfwd) twice, K2tog tbl, rep from * to last 0 (1: 1: 0: 0) st, K0 (1: 1: 0: 0).

Row 2: P1 (2: 2: 1: 1), *(P1, P1 tbl) into double yfwd of previous row, cluster 2, rep from * to last 3 (4: 4: 3: 3) sts, (P1, P1 tbl) into double yfwd of previous row, P1 (2: 2: 1: 1).

Row 3: K2 (3: 3: 2: 2), *K2tog, (yfwd) twice, K2tog tbl, rep from * to last 2 (3: 3: 2: 2) sts, K2 (3: 3: 2: 2).

Row 4: P1 (2: 2: 1: 1), *cluster 2, (P1, P1 tbl) into double yfwd of previous row, rep from * to last 3 (4: 4: 3: 3) sts, cluster 2, P1 (2: 2: 1: 1).

These 4 rows form patt.

Cont in patt for a further 2 rows, ending with a WS row.

Change to 12mm (US 17) needles.

Keeping patt correct, dec 1 st at each end of next and every foll 4th row until 44 (46: 50: 52: 56) sts rem.

Work 5 rows, ending with a WS row.

Inc 1 st at each end of next and foll 6th row, then on every foll 4th row until there are 52 (54: 58: 60: 64) sts, taking inc sts into patt.

Cont straight until back measures 35 (36: 36: 37: 37) cm, ending with a WS row.

Shape armholes

Keeping patt correct, cast off 3 sts at beg of next 2 rows. 46 (48: 52: 54: 58) sts.

Dec 1 st at each end of next 1 (3: 3: 5: 5) rows, then on foll 2 (1: 2: 1: 2) alt rows. 40 (40: 42: 42: 44) sts.

Cont straight until armhole measures 20 (20: 21: 21: 22) cm, ending with a WS row.

Shape shoulders and back neck

Cast off 4 sts at beg of next 2 rows. 32 (32: 34: 34: 36) sts.

Next row (RS): Cast off 4 sts, patt until there are 5 (5: 6: 5: 6) sts on right needle and turn, leaving rem sts on a holder.

Work each side of neck separately.

Cast off 2 sts at beg of next row.

Cast off rem 3 (3: 4: 3: 4) sts.

With RS facing, rejoin yarn to rem sts, cast off centre 14 (14: 14: 16: 16) sts, patt to end.

Complete to match first side, reversing shapings.

LEFT FRONT

Cast on 29 (30: 32: 33: 35) sts using 10mm (US 15) needles.

Row 1 (RS): K0 (1: 1: 0: 0), *K2tog, (yfwd) twice, K2tog tbl, rep from * to last 1 (1: 3: 1: 3) sts, K1 (1: 3: 1: 3).

Row 2: K1, P1 (1: 3: 1: 3), *(P1, P1 tbl) into double yfwd of previous row, cluster 2, rep from * to last 3 (4: 4: 3: 3) sts, (P1, P1 tbl) into double yfwd of previous row, P1 (2: 2: 1: 1).

Row 3: K2 (3: 3: 2: 2), *K2tog, (yfwd) twice, K2tog tbl, rep from * to last 3 (3: 1: 3: 1) sts, K3 (3: 1: 3: 1).

Row 4: K1, P1 (1: 3: 1: 3), *cluster 2, (P1, P1 tbl) into double yfwd of previous row, rep from * to last 3 (4: 4: 3: 3) sts, cluster 2, P1 (2: 2: 1: 1).

These 4 rows form patt.

Cont in patt for a further 2 rows, ending with a WS row.

Change to 12mm (US 17) needles.

Keeping patt correct, dec 1 st at beg of next and foll 4th row until 25 (26: 28: 29: 31) sts rem.

Work 5 rows, ending with a WS row.

Inc 1 st at beg of next and foll 6th row, then on every foll 4th row until there are 29 (30: 32: 33: 35) sts, taking inc sts into patt.

Cont straight until left front matches back to beg of armhole shaping, ending with a WS row.

Shape armhole

Keeping patt correct, cast off 3 sts at beg of next row. 26 (27: 29: 30: 32) sts.

Work 1 row.

Dec 1 st at armhole edge of next 1 (3: 3: 5: 5) rows, then on foll 2 (1: 2: 1: 2) alt rows. 23 (23: 24: 24: 25) sts.

Cont straight until 9 (9: 9: 11: 11) rows less have been worked than on back to start of shoulder shaping, ending with a RS row.

Shape neck

Keeping patt correct, cast off 6 sts at beg of next row.

17 (17: 18: 18: 19) sts.

Dec 1 st at neck edge of next 4 rows, then on foll 2 (2: 2: 3: 3) alt rows, ending with a WS row. 11 (11: 12: 11: 12) sts.

Shape shoulder

Cast off 4 sts at beg of next and foll alt row.

Work 1 row.

Cast off rem 3 (3: 4: 3: 4) sts.

RIGHT FRONT

Cast on 29 (30: 32: 33: 35) sts using 10mm (US 15) needles.

Row 1 (RS): K1 (1: 3: 1: 3), *K2tog, (yfwd) twice, K2tog tbl, rep from * to last 0 (1: 1: 0: 0) sts, K0 (1: 1: 0: 0).

Row 2: P1 (2: 2: 1: 1), (P1, P1 tbl) into double yfwd of previous row, *cluster 2, (P1, P1 tbl) into double yfwd of previous row, rep from * to last 2 (2: 4: 2: 4) sts, P1 (1: 3: 1: 3), K1.

Row 3: K3 (3: 1: 3: 1), *K2tog, (yfwd) twice, K2tog tbl, rep from * to last 2 (3: 3: 2: 2) sts, K2 (3: 3: 2: 2).

Row 4: P1 (2: 2: 1: 1), cluster 2, *(P1, P1 tbl) into double yfwd of previous row, cluster 2, rep from * to last 2 (2: 4: 2: 4) sts, P1 (1: 3: 1: 3), K1.

These 4 rows form patt.

Cont in patt for a further 2 rows, ending with a WS row.

Change to 12mm (US 17) needles.

Keeping patt correct, dec 1 st at end of next and every foll 4th row until 25 (26: 28: 29: 31) sts rem.

Complete to match left front, reversing shapings.

SLEEVES (both alike)

Cast on 42 (42: 44: 44: 46) sts using 10mm (US 15) needles.

Row 1 (RS): K1 (1: 0: 0: 1), *K2tog, (yfwd) twice, K2tog tbl, rep from * to last 1 (1: 0: 0: 1) st, K1 (1: 0: 0: 1).

Row 2: P2 (2: 1: 1: 2), *(P1, P1 tbl) into double yfwd of previous row, cluster 2, rep from * to last 4 (4: 3: 3: 4) sts, (P1, P1 tbl) into double yfwd of previous row, P2 (2: 1: 1: 2).

Row 3: K3 (3: 2: 2: 3), *K2tog, (yfwd) twice, K2tog tbl, rep from * to last 3 (3: 2: 2: 3) sts, K3 (3: 2: 2: 3).

Row 4: P2 (2: 1: 1: 2), *cluster 2, (P1, P1 tbl) into double yfwd of previous row, rep from * to last 4 (4: 3: 3: 4) sts, cluster 2, P2 (2: 1: 1: 2).

These 4 rows form patt.

Cont in patt for a further 2 rows, ending with a WS row.

Change to 12mm (US 17) needles.

Cont in patt until sleeve measures 43 (43: 44: 44: 44) cm, ending with a WS row.

Shape top

Keeping patt correct, cast off 3 sts at beg of next 2 rows.

36 (36: 38: 38: 40) sts.

Dec 1 st at each end of next 3 rows, then on foll alt row, then on foll 4th row.

26 (26: 28: 28: 30) sts.

Work 1 row, ending with a WS row.

Dec 1 st at each end of next and every foll alt row to 20 sts, then on foll row, ending with a WS row.

Cast off rem 18 sts.

MAKING UP

PRESS as described on the information page. Join both shoulder seams using back stitch, or mattress stitch if preferred.

Neckband

With RS facing and using 7mm (US 10½) needles, starting and ending at front opening edges, pick up and knit 19 (19: 19: 21: 21) sts up right side of neck, 18 (18: 18: 20: 20) sts from back, then 19 (19: 19: 21: 21) sts down left side of neck. 56 (56: 56: 62: 62) sts.

Cast off knitwise (on WS).

See information page for finishing instructions, setting in sleeves using the set-in method.

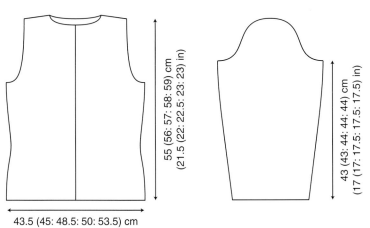

55 (56: 57: 58: 59) cm
(21.5 (22: 22.5: 23: 23) in)

43 (43: 44: 44: 44) cm
(17 (17: 17.5: 17.5: 17.5) in)

43.5 (45: 48.5: 50: 53.5) cm
(17 (17.5: 19: 19.5: 21) in)

DIXIE

KIM HARGREAVES

YARN

Rowan Chunky Print

3 x 100gm
(photographed in Shriek 001 and Woolly 071)

NEEDLES

1 pair 8mm (no 0) (US 11) needles
1 pair 12mm (US 17) needles
2 double-pointed 8mm (no 0) (US 11) needles

TENSION

10 sts and 14½ rows to 10 cm measured over pattern using 8mm (US 11) and 12mm (US 17) needles.

FINISHED SIZE

Completed scarf measures 15 cm (6 in) wide and 200 cm (78½ in) long (excluding fringe).

FRINGE STRIP (make 18)

Cast on 3 sts using double-pointed 8mm (US 11) needles.

Row 1 (RS): K3, ★without turning work slip these 3 sts to opposite end of needle and bring yarn to opposite end of work pulling it quite tightly across back of these 3 sts, using other needle K these 3 sts again; rep from ★ until strip is 20 cm long, break yarn and leave sts on a holder.

Cont in this way, making a further 17 fringe strips and leaving yarn attached to 2 of these strips.

SCARF

First section

Using 8mm (US 11) needles and yarn attached to one fringe strip, K across the 3 sts of this fringe strip, (K across 3 sts of next fringe strip) 4 times.

15 sts.

Work in garter st for 5 rows, ending with a WS row.

Row 6 (RS): ★K1, (holding a fringe strip against RS of scarf, K tog first st of fringe strip with next st of scarf, K tog rem 2 sts of same fringe strip with next 2 sts of scarf) twice, rep from ★ once more, K1.

Row 7. Knit.

Cont in patt as folls:

Rows 1 to 4: Using 8mm (US 11) needles, knit.

Row 5: Using 12mm (US 17) needles, knit.

Row 6: Using 12mm (US 17) needles, purl.

These 6 rows form patt.

Cont in patt until first section measures 100 cm from where first set of fringe strips are joined, ending with a WS row.★★

Break yarn and leave sts on a holder.

Second section

Work as given for first section to ★★.

Join sections

Holding sections RS together, cast off sts of both sections together.

MAKING UP

PRESS as described on the information page.

No 7

FIFI

KIM HARGREAVES

YARN

Rowan Chunky Print
3 x 100gm
(photographed in Native 072)

CROCHET HOOK

6.00mm (no 4) (US J10) crochet hook
9.00mm (no 00) crochet hook

EXTRAS

1 m of 5-6mm diameter plastic tubing and strong cord or elastic for handles

TENSION

2 pattern repeats and 8 rows to 10 cm measured over pattern using 9.00mm crochet hook.

FINISHED SIZE

Completed bag measures 24 cm (9½ in) wide and 23 cm (9 in) deep (excluding fringe).

CROCHET ABBREVIATIONS

ch = chain; **ss** = slip stitch;
dc = double crochet; **tr** = treble.

SIDES (make 2)

Using 9.00mm hook, make 32 ch.
Row 1 (RS): 1 dc into 2nd ch from hook, ★miss 2 ch, 5 tr into next ch, miss 2 ch, 1 dc into next ch, rep from ★ to end, turn. 31 sts, 5 patt reps.
Row 2: 3 ch (counts as first tr), 2 tr into dc at end of previous row, ★miss 2 tr, 1 dc into next tr, miss 2 tr★★, 5 tr into next dc, rep from ★ to end, ending last rep at ★★, 3 tr into next dc, turn.
Row 3: 1 ch (does NOT count as st), 1 dc into tr at end of previous row, ★miss 2 tr, 5 tr into next dc, miss 2 tr, 1 dc into next tr, rep from ★ to end, working dc at end of last rep into top of 3 ch at beg of previous row, turn.
Last 2 rows form patt.
Work a further 14 rows, ending with a RS row.
Next row (WS): 3 ch (counts as first tr), miss dc at end of previous row, miss 1 tr, 1 tr into each of next 4 tr, miss 1 dc, ★1 tr into each of next 5 tr, miss 1 dc, rep from ★ to end, turn. 25 sts.
Next row: 3 ch (counts as first tr), 1 tr into

each tr to end, working last tr into top of 3 ch at beg of previous row, turn.
Rep last row once more.
Fasten off.

HANDLES (make 2)

Cut a 45 cm length of plastic tubing. Thread a length of strong cord or elastic through tubing and tie ends together securely, pulling tubing round so that it forms a ring.
Using 6.00mm (US J10) hook, work one round of dc over tubing so that tubing is completely covered, ending with ss to first dc.
Fasten off.

MAKING UP

PRESS as described on the information page.
Join sides along side and lower edges, leaving 12 cm open at top of each side seam. Wrap last few rows of sides over handles and stitch in place.
Fringe
Cut 40 lengths of yarn, each 30 cm long.
Knot centre of each length of yarn to inside of base seam and then thread ends through to RS to form a fringe. Trim ends.

No 8

FANNY

KIM HARGREAVES

YARN

	XS	S	M	L	XL	
To fit bust	81	86	91	97	102	cm
	32	34	36	38	40	in

Rowan Big Wool

	9	10	10	11	12	x 100gm

(photographed in Tricky 030)

NEEDLES

1 pair 10mm (no 000) (US 15) needles
1 pair 12mm (US 17) needles
Cable needle

BUTTONS

4 x 00358

TENSION

8 sts and 12 rows to 10 cm measured over
stocking stitch using 12mm (US 17) needles.

SPECIAL ABBREVIATIONS

C3B = slip next st onto cable needle and
leave at back of work, K2, then K1 from cable
needle.
C3F = slip next 2 sts onto cable needle and
leave at front of work, K1, then K2 from cable
needle.
C4B = slip next 2 sts onto cable needle and
leave at back of work, K2, then K2 from cable
needle.
C4F = slip next 2 sts onto cable needle and
leave at front of work, K2, then K2 from cable
needle.

BACK

Cast on 46 (48: 50: 52: 54) sts using 12mm
(US 17) needles.
Row 1 (RS): Knit.

Row 2: P0 (0: 1: 2: 3), K1 (2: 2: 2: 2), (P3, K2)
twice, (P2, K2) twice, (P3, K2) twice, (P2, K2)
twice, P3, K2, P3, K1 (2: 2: 2: 2), P0 (0: 1: 2: 3).
These 2 rows form rib.
Work in rib for a further 6 rows, ending with
a WS row.
Cont in cable patt as folls:
Row 1 (RS): K11 (12: 13: 14: 15), C3F, C3B,
K12, C3F, C3B, K to end.
Row 2: P9 (10: 11: 12: 13), K3, P4, K3, P8,
K3, P4, K3, P to end.
Row 3: K12 (13: 14: 15: 16), C4B, K14, C4F,
K to end.
Row 4: As row 2.
Row 5: K2, K2tog, K to last 4 sts, K2tog tbl,
K2. 44 (46: 48: 50: 52) sts.
Row 6: P8 (9: 10: 11: 12), K3, P4, K3, P8, K3,
P4, K3, P to end.
Row 7: Knit.
Row 8: As row 6.
Row 9: K11 (12: 13: 14: 15), C4B, K14, C4F,
K to end.
Row 10: As row 6.
Row 11: K2, K2tog, K6 (7: 8: 9: 10), C3B,
C3F, K12, C3B, C3F, K to last 4 sts, K2tog tbl,
K2. 42 (44: 46: 48: 50) sts.
Row 12: P7 (8: 9: 10: 11), (K2, P2) twice, K2,
P8, (K2, P2) twice, K2, P to end.
Row 13: Knit.
Rows 14 and 15: As rows 12 and 13.
Row 16: As row 12.
Row 17: As row 5. 40 (42: 44: 46: 48) sts.
Row 18: P6 (7: 8: 9: 10), (K2, P2) twice, K2,
P8, (K2, P2) twice, K2, P to end.
Row 19: Knit.
Row 20: As row 18.
Last 20 rows set the sts - 2 cable panels with st st
between and at sides - and start side seam shaping.

Cont as set for a further 4 rows, ending with a
WS row.
Next row (RS): K2, M1, patt to last 2 sts,
M1, K2. 42 (44: 46: 48: 50) sts.
Working all increases as set by last row, inc 1 st
at each end of 6th and foll 6th row, taking inc
sts into st st. 46 (48: 50: 52: 54) sts.
Cont straight until back measures 43 (44: 44:
45: 45) cm, ending with a WS row.
Shape armholes
Keeping patt correct, cast off 2 sts at beg of
next 2 rows. 42 (44: 46: 48: 50) sts.
Dec 1 st at each end of next 3 (3: 4: 4: 5)
rows, then on foll 2 alt rows.
32 (34: 34: 36: 36) sts.
Cont straight until armhole measures 20 (20:
21: 21: 22) cm, ending with a WS row.
Shape shoulders and back neck
Next row (RS): Cast off 5 sts, patt until
there are 7 (8: 8: 8: 8) sts on right needle and
turn, leaving rem sts on a holder.
Work each side of neck separately.
Cast off 2 sts at beg of next row.
Cast off rem 5 (6: 6: 6: 6) sts.
With RS facing, rejoin yarn to rem sts, cast off
centre 8 (8: 8: 10: 10) sts, patt to end.
Complete to match first side, reversing
shapings.

LEFT FRONT

Cast on 26 (27: 28: 29: 30) sts using 12mm
(US 17) needles.
Row 1 (RS): Knit.
Row 2: K4, P3, (K2, P2) twice, (K2, P3)
twice, K1 (2: 2: 2: 2), P0 (0: 1: 2: 3).
These 2 rows form rib.
Work in rib for a further 6 rows, ending with
a WS row.

Cont in cable patt as folls:

Row 1 (RS): K11 (12: 13: 14: 15), C3F, C3B, K to end.

Row 2: K4, P3, K3, P4, K3, P to end.

Row 3: K12 (13: 14: 15: 16), C4B, K to end.

Row 4: As row 2.

Row 5: K2, K2tog, K to end. 25 (26: 27: 28: 29) sts.

Row 6: As row 2.

Row 7: Knit.

Row 8: As row 2.

Row 9: K11 (12: 13: 14: 15), C4B, K to end.

Row 10: As row 2.

Row 11: K2, K2tog, K6 (7: 8: 9: 10), C3B, C3F, K to end. 24 (25: 26: 27: 28) sts.

Row 12: K4, P3, (K2, P2) twice, K2, P to end.

Row 13: Knit.

Rows 14 and 15: As rows 12 and 13.

Row 16: As row 12.

Row 17: As row 5. 23 (24: 25: 26: 27) sts.

Row 18: As row 12.

Row 19: Knit.

Row 20: As row 12.

Last 20 rows set the sts – cable panel with st st either side and front opening edge garter st border - and start side seam shaping.

Cont as set for a further 4 rows, ending with a WS row.

Next row (RS): K2, M1, patt to end. 24 (25: 26: 27: 28) sts.

Working all increases as set by last row, inc 1 st at beg of 6th and foll 6th row, taking inc sts into st st. 26 (27: 28: 29: 30) sts.

Cont straight until left front matches back to beg of armhole shaping, ending with a WS row.

Shape armhole

Keeping patt correct, cast off 2 sts at beg of next row. 24 (25: 26: 27: 28) sts.

Work 1 row.

Dec 1 st at armhole edge of next 3 (3: 4: 4: 5) rows, then on foll 2 alt rows. 19 (20: 20: 21: 21) sts.

Cont straight until 8 rows less have been worked than on back to start of shoulder shaping, ending with a WS row.

Shape neck

Next row (RS): Patt 15 (16: 16: 16: 16) sts and turn, leaving rem 4 (4: 4: 5: 5) sts on a holder.

Dec 1 st at neck edge on next 5 rows. 10 (11: 11: 11: 11) sts.

Work 2 rows, ending with a WS row.

Shape shoulder

Cast off 5 sts at beg of next row.

Work 1 row.

Cast off rem 5 (6: 6: 6: 6) sts.

Mark positions for 4 buttons along left front opening edge – first to come level with row 11, last to come 3 cm below neck shaping, and rem 2 buttons evenly spaced between.

RIGHT FRONT

Cast on 26 (27: 28: 29: 30) sts using 12mm (US 17) needles.

Row 1 (RS): Knit.

Row 2: P0 (0: 1: 2: 3), K1 (2: 2: 2: 2), (P3, K2) twice, (P2, K2) twice, P3, K4.

These 2 rows form rib.

Work in rib for a further 6 rows, ending with a WS row.

Cont in cable patt as folls:

Row 1 (RS): K9, C3F, C3B, K to end.

Row 2: P9 (10: 11: 12: 13), K3, P4, K3, P3, K4.

Row 3 (buttonhole row): K1, K2tog, yfwd (to make a buttonhole), K7, C4F, K to end.

Making a further 3 buttonholes in this way to correspond with positions marked for buttons on left front and noting that no further reference will be made to buttonholes, cont as folls:

Row 4: As row 2.

Row 5: K to last 4 sts, K2tog tbl, K2. 25 (26: 27: 28: 29) sts.

Row 6: P to last 17 sts, K3, P4, K3, P3, K4.

Row 7: Knit.

Row 8: As row 6.

Row 9: K10, C4F, K to end.

Row 10: As row 6.

Row 11: K9, C3B, C3F, K to last 4 sts, K2tog tbl, K2. 24 (25: 26: 27: 28) sts.

Row 12: P to last 17 sts, (K2, P2) twice, K2, P3, K4.

Row 13: Knit.

Rows 14 and 15: As rows 12 and 13.

Row 16: As row 12.

Row 17: As row 5. 23 (24: 25: 26: 27) sts.

Row 18: As row 12.

Row 19: Knit.

Row 20: As row 12.

Last 20 rows set the sts – cable panel with st st either side and front opening edge garter st border - and start side seam shaping.

Complete to match left front, reversing shapings and working first row of neck shaping as folls:

Shape neck

Next row (RS): Patt 4 (4: 4: 5: 5) sts and slip these sts onto a holder, patt to end. 15 (16: 16: 16: 16) sts.

LEFT SLEEVE

Cast on 28 (28: 28: 30: 30) sts using 12mm (US 17) needles.

Row 1 (RS): Knit.

Row 2: K1 (1: 1: 2: 2), (P3, K2) twice, (P2, K2) twice, P3, K2, P3, K1 (1: 1: 2: 2).

These 2 rows form rib.

Work in rib for a further 12 rows, ending with a WS row.

Row 15 (RS): K11 (11: 11: 12: 12), C3F, C3B, K to end.

Row 16: K1 (1: 1: 2: 2), P3, K2, P3, K3, P4, K3, P3, K2, P3, K1 (1: 1: 2: 2).

Row 17: K12 (12: 12: 13: 13), C4F, K to end.

Row 18: P9 (9: 9: 10: 10), K3, P4, K3, P to end.

Last 2 rows set the sts – cable panel as given for back with st st at either side.

Working increases in same way as given for side seam increases, cont in patt as now set, shaping sides by inc 1 st at each end of 19th (19th: 13th: 19th: 13th) and foll 0 (0: 12th: 0: 12th) row. 30 (30: 32: 32: 34) sts.

Cont straight until sleeve measures 43 (43: 44: 44: 44) cm, ending with a WS row.

Shape top

Keeping patt correct, cast off 2 sts at beg of next 2 rows. 26 (26: 28: 28: 30) sts.

Dec 1 st at each end of next and foll alt row, then on foll 4th row, then on every foll alt row to 16 sts, then on foll 3 rows, ending with a WS row. Cast off rem 10 sts.

RIGHT SLEEVE

Work as given for left sleeve but replacing "C4F" with "C4B".

MAKING UP

PRESS as described on the information page. Join both shoulder seams using back stitch, or mattress stitch if preferred.

Collar

With RS facing and using 12mm (US 17) needles, slip 4 (4: 4: 5: 5) sts from right front holder onto right needle, rejoin yarn and pick up and knit 11 sts up right side of neck, 17 (17: 17: 18: 18) sts from back, 11 sts down left side of neck, then patt across 4 (4: 4: 5: 5) sts on left front holder.
47 (47: 47: 50: 50) sts.

Row 1 (WS of body, RS of collar): Knit.
Row 2: K4, (P3, K2) twice, (P1, K2) 7 (7: 7: 8: 8) times, P3, K2, P3, K4.
Rows 3 and 4: As rows 1 and 2.
Row 5: K14, (M1, K1, M1, K2) 7 (7: 7: 8: 8) times, K to end.
61 (61: 61: 66: 66) sts.

Row 6: K4, ★P3, K2, rep from ★ to last 7 sts, P3, K4.
Row 7: Knit.
Rep last 2 rows until collar measures 25 cm, ending with a WS row.
Cast off.

Belt

Cast on 6 sts using 10mm (US 15) needles. Work in garter st until belt measures 130 cm. Cast off.

See information page for finishing instructions, setting in sleeves using the set-in method.

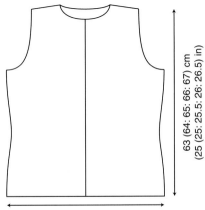

63 (64: 65: 66: 67) cm
(25 (25: 25.5: 26: 26.5) in)

52.5 (55: 57.5: 60: 62.5) cm
(20.5 (21.5: 22.5: 23.5: 24.5) in)

43 (43: 44: 44: 44) cm
(17 (17: 17.5: 17.5: 17.5) in)

No 9

FLOSS

KIM HARGREAVES

YARN

	XS-S	S-M	M-L	L-XL	
To fit bust	81-86	86-91	91-97	97-102	cm
	32-34	34-36	36-38	38-40	in

Rowan Chunky Print
A Chunky Print Native 072
                3   3   4   4 x 100gm
B Biggy Print   Glum   244
                1   1   1   1 x 100gm

NEEDLES

1 pair 8mm (no 0) (US 11) needles

TENSION

11 sts and 14 rows to 10 cm measured over stocking stitch using 8mm (US 11) needles.

BACK and FRONT
(both alike – knitted downwards)

Cast on 44 (48: 52: 56) sts using 8mm (US 11) needles and yarn A.
Row 1 (RS): P3, ★K2, P2, rep from ★ to last st, P1.
Row 2: K3, ★P2, K2, rep from ★ to last st, K1.
These 2 rows form rib.
Cont in rib for a further 12 rows, ending with a WS row.
Row 15 (RS): P2, K2tog, rib to last 4 sts, K2tog tbl, P2. 42 (46: 50: 54) sts.

Work 7 rows.
Row 23: As row 15. 40 (44: 48: 50) sts.
Work 5 rows.
Row 29: P2, P2tog, rib to last 4 sts, P2tog tbl, P2. 38 (42: 46: 50) sts.
Cont straight until work measures 27 (27: 28: 28) cm, ending with a WS row.
Next row (RS): P2, M1, rib to last 2 sts, M1, P2.
Working all increases as set by last row and taking inc sts into rib, inc 1 st at each end of 8th and foll 6th row. 44 (48: 52: 56) sts.
Cont straight until work measures 46 (46: 47: 47) cm, ending with a WS row.
Cast off in rib.

MAKING UP

PRESS as described on the information page. Join both side seams using back stitch, or mattress stitch if preferred.
Embroidery
Using photograph as a guide and yarn B DOUBLE, embroider a cross st on the K sts of one line of rib to the left of centre front and near lower (cast-**off**) edge at folls: take yarn to WS at lower right corner of cross and bring it back to RS in lower left corner. Take it back to WS in upper right corner and bring it back to RS in upper left corner. Take yarn to WS in lower right corner, then bring it back to RS in lower left corner. Leave ends free on RS, trimming them to approx 12-17 cm. Make another cross st on same rib directly above first. Start a third cross st on same rib, but this time cont in cross st up this rib to upper edge. On the P sts next to this decorated rib (working towards side seam), embroider 3 more cross sts, staggering them slightly in relation to first set of cross sts. On the K sts next to these sts (working towards side seam), embroider a further one cross st and then a line of cross st up to upper edge.

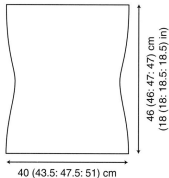

46 (46: 47: 47) cm
(18 (18: 18.5: 18.5) in)

40 (43.5: 47.5: 51) cm
(15.5 (17: 18.5: 20) in)

No 10

ROXIE

KIM HARGREAVES

YARN

	XS	S	M	L	XL	
To fit bust	81	86	91	97	102	cm
	32	34	36	38	40	in

Rowan Chunky Print

| | 8 | 8 | 9 | 9 | 10 | x 100gm |

(photographed in Pit 080)

NEEDLES

1 pair 8mm (no 0) (US 11) needles

FASTENER – 1 large hook and eye

TENSION

11 sts and 14 rows to 10 cm measured over stocking stitch using 8mm (US 11) needles.

SPECIAL ABBREVIATIONS

Loop 1 = K next st leaving st on left needle, bring yarn to RS of work between needles and wrap it twice round thumb of left hand, take yarn back to WS of work between needles and K same st again, slipping it off left needle. Bring yarn forward between needles and take it back over right needle, then lift 2 sts just made over this loop and off right needle.

BACK

Cast on 51 (53: 57: 59: 63) sts using 8mm (US 11) needles.
Work in garter st for 2 rows, ending with a WS row.
Row 3 (RS): K1, *loop 1, K1, rep from * to end.
Row 4: Knit.
Row 5: K2, *loop 1, K1, rep from * to last st, K1.

Row 6: Knit.
Rows 7 to 10: As rows 3 to 6.
Row 11: As row 3.
Row 12: Purl.
These 12 rows complete fur st border.
Beg with a K row, cont in st st as folls:
Work 2 rows, ending with a WS row.
Next row (RS): K2, K2tog, K to last 4 sts, K2tog tbl, K2.
Working all decreases as set by last row, dec 1 st at each end of 6th and every foll 4th row until 43 (45: 49: 51: 55) sts rem.
Cont straight until back measures 23 (24: 24: 25: 25) cm, ending with a WS row.
Next row (RS): K2, M1, K to last 2 sts, M1, K2.
Working all increases as set by last row, inc 1 st at each end of every foll 6th row until there are 51 (53: 57: 59: 63) sts.
Work a further 5 rows, ending with a WS row.
(Back should measure 40 (41: 41: 42: 42) cm.)
Shape armholes
Cast off 3 sts at beg of next 2 rows.
45 (47: 51: 53: 57) sts.
Dec 1 st at each end of next 1 (3: 3: 5: 5) rows, then on foll 2 (1: 2: 1: 2) alt rows.
39 (39: 41: 41: 43) sts.
Cont straight until armhole measures 20 (20: 21: 21: 22) cm, ending with a WS row.
Shape shoulders and back neck
Next row (RS): Cast off 4 sts, K until there are 9 (9: 10: 9: 10) sts on right needle and turn, leaving rem sts on a holder.
Work each side of neck separately.
Dec 1 st at beg of next row.
Cast off 4 sts at beg and dec 1 st at end of next row.
Work 1 row.

Cast off rem 3 (3: 4: 3: 4) sts.
With RS facing, rejoin yarn to rem sts, cast off centre 13 (13: 13: 15: 15) sts, K to end.
Complete to match first side, reversing shapings.

LEFT FRONT

Cast on 28 (29: 31: 32: 34) sts using 8mm (US 11) needles.
Work in garter st for 2 rows, ending with a WS row.
Row 3 (RS): *K1, loop 1, rep from * to last 2 (1: 1: 2: 2) sts, K2 (1: 1: 2: 2).
Row 4: Knit.
Row 5: K2, *loop 1, K1, rep from * to last 0 (1: 1: 0: 0) st, K0 (1: 1: 0: 0).
Row 6: Knit.
Rows 7 to 10: As rows 3 to 6.
Row 11: As row 3.
Row 12: K6, P to end.
These 12 rows complete fur st border.
Cont in st st with fur st border along front opening edge as folls:
Next row (RS): K to last 6 sts, patt 6 sts.
Next row: K6, P to end.
These 2 rows set the sts – front opening edge 6 sts still in fur st with rem sts in st st.
Keeping sts correct as set and working all side seam decreases and increases in same way as for back, cont as folls:
Dec 1 st at beg of next and foll 6th row, then on every foll 4th row until 24 (25: 27: 28: 30) sts rem.
Cont straight until left front measures 23 (24: 24: 25: 25) cm, ending with a WS row.
Inc 1 st at beg of next row.
25 (26: 28: 29: 31) sts.
Work 5 rows, ending with a WS row.

Shape front slope

Next row (RS): K2, M1, K to last 9 sts, K2tog tbl, K1, patt 6 sts. 25 (26: 28: 29: 31) sts.
Working all front slope decreases as set by last row, inc 1 st at side seam edge of 6th and foll 6th row **and at same time** dec 1 st at front slope edge on 12th (12th: 12th: 8th: 8th) row. 26 (27: 29: 30: 32) sts.
Work a further 5 rows, ending with a WS row. (Left front now matches back to beg of armhole shaping.)

Shape armhole

Cast off 3 sts at beg and dec 0 (0: 0: 1: 1) st at front slope edge of next row.
23 (24: 26: 26: 28) sts.
Work 1 row.
Dec 1 st at armhole edge of next 1 (3: 3: 5: 5) rows, then on foll 2 (1: 2: 1: 2) alt rows **and at same time** dec 1 st at front slope edge on 5th (5th: 5th: 0: 9th) row.
19 (19: 20: 20: 20) sts.
Dec 1 st at front slope edge **only** on 12th (12th: 12th: 2nd: 10th) and foll 0 (0: 0: 10th: 0) row. 18 (18: 19: 18: 19) sts.
Cont straight until left front matches back to start of shoulder shaping, ending with a WS row.

Shape shoulder

Cast off 4 sts at beg of next and foll alt row, then 3 (3: 4: 3: 4) sts at beg of foll alt row.
Work a further 7.5 (7.5: 7.5: 8.5: 8.5) cm on rem 7 sts for back neck border extension, ending with a WS row.
Cast off.

RIGHT FRONT

Cast on 28 (29: 31: 32: 34) sts using 8mm (US 11) needles.
Work in garter st for 2 rows, ending with a WS row.
Row 3 (RS): K2 (1: 1: 2: 2), *loop 1, K1, rep from * to end.
Row 4: Knit.
Row 5: K0 (1: 1: 0: 0), *K1, loop 1, rep from * to last 2 sts, K2.
Row 6: Knit.
Rows 7 to 10: As rows 3 to 6.

Row 11: As row 3.
Row 12: P to last 6 sts, K6.
These 12 rows complete fur st border.
Cont in st st with fur st border along front opening edge as folls:
Next row (RS): Patt 6 sts, K to end.
Next row: P to last 6 sts, K6.
These 2 rows set the sts – front opening edge 6 sts still in fur st with rem sts in st st.
Keeping sts correct as set and working all side seam decreases and increases in same way as for back, complete to match left front, reversing shapings.

SLEEVES (both alike)

Cast on 35 (35: 37: 37: 39) sts using 8mm (US 11) needles.
Work in garter st for 2 rows, ending with a WS row.
Row 3 (RS): K1, *loop 1, K1, rep from * to end.
Row 4: Knit.
Row 5: K2, *loop 1, K1, rep from * to last st, K1.
Row 6: Knit.
Rows 7 to 18: As rows 3 to 6, 3 times.
Row 19: As row 3.
Row 20: Purl.
These 20 rows complete fur st border.
Beg with a K row and working all increases in same way as for side seam increases, cont in st st, shaping sides by inc 1 st at each end of 11th and foll 20th row.
39 (39: 41: 41: 43) sts.
Cont straight until sleeve measures 43 (43: 44: 44: 44) cm, ending with a WS row.

Shape top

Cast off 3 sts at beg of next 2 rows.
33 (33: 35: 35: 37) sts.
Dec 1 st at each end of next 3 rows, then on foll alt row, then on foll 4th row.
23 (23: 25: 25: 27) sts.
Work 3 rows, ending with a WS row.
Dec 1 st at each end of next and every foll alt row to 19 sts, then on foll 3 rows, ending with a WS row.
Cast off rem 13 sts.

PRESS as described on the information page. Join both shoulder seams using back stitch, or mattress stitch if preferred. Join cast-off ends of back neck border extensions, then sew one edge to back neck.
See information page for finishing instructions, setting in sleeves using the set-in method. Attach hook eye to inside of front opening edges level with start of front slope shaping.
If desired, carefully snip each loop of fur st borders and lightly brush area to create a shaggy effect.

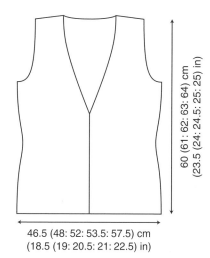

46.5 (48: 52: 53.5: 57.5) cm
(18.5 (19: 20.5: 21: 22.5) in)

60 (61: 62: 63: 64) cm
(23.5 (24: 24.5: 25: 25) in)

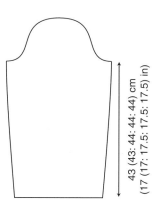

43 (43: 44: 44: 44) cm
(17 (17: 17.5: 17.5: 17.5) in)

No 11

VIRGINA

LEAH SUTTON

YARN

	XS	S	M	L	XL	
To fit bust	81	86	91	97	102	cm
	32	34	36	38	40	in

Rowan Chunky Print and Big Wool Tuft
A Print Woolly 071 5 5 6 6 6 x 100gm
B Tuft Frosty 055 3 3 3 4 4 x 50gm

NEEDLES

1 pair 9mm (no 00) (US 13) needles
1 pair 20mm (US 36) needles

TENSION

Chunky Print: 11 sts and 16 rows to 10 cm measured over moss stitch using 9mm (US 13) needles.
Big Wool Tuft: 5½ sts and 7 rows to 10 cm measured over stocking stitch using 20mm (US 36) needles.

BACK

Cast on 45 (47: 51: 53: 57) sts using 9mm (US 13) needles and yarn A.
Row 1 (RS): K1, *P1, K1, rep from * to end.
Row 2: As row 1.
These 2 rows form moss st.
Cont in moss st until back measures 26 cm, ending with a WS row.
Shape armholes
Keeping moss st correct, cast off 4 sts at beg of next 2 rows. 37 (39: 43: 45: 49) sts.
Dec 1 st at each end of next and foll 0 (1: 4: 4: 7) alt rows, then on every foll 4th row until 21 (21: 21: 23: 23) sts rem.
Work 3 (1: 1: 1: 1) rows, ending with a WS row.
Shape back neck
Next row (RS): Moss st 6 sts and turn, leaving rem sts on a holder.

Work each side of neck separately.
Cast off 3 sts at beg of next row.
Cast off rem 3 sts.
With RS facing, rejoin yarn to rem sts, cast off centre 9 (9: 9: 11: 11) sts, moss st to end.
Complete to match first side, reversing shapings.

FRONT

Cast on 23 (25: 27: 27: 29) sts loosely using 20mm (US 36) needles and yarn B, taking time to pull "tufts" of yarn through sts.
Beg with a K row, cont in st st until front measures 23 cm, ending with a WS row.
Divide for neck
Next row (RS): K9 (10: 11: 11: 12), K2tog, K1 and turn, leaving rem sts on a holder.
11 (12: 13: 13: 14) sts.
Work each side of neck separately.
Working a slip st edging as described on the information page at neck edge (end of RS rows and beg of WS rows), cont as folls:
Work 1 row. (Front should now match back to beg of armhole shaping.)
Shape armhole
Cast off 2 sts at beg of next row.
9 (10: 11: 11: 12) sts.
Work 1 row.
Next row (RS): K2tog, K to last 3 sts, K2tog, patt 1 st. 7 (8: 9: 9: 10) sts.
Working all neck decreases as set by last row, cont as folls:
Dec 1 st at armhole edge of 4th (2nd: 2nd: 2nd: 2nd) and foll 0 (0: 2: 2: 3) alt rows, then on 1 (2: 1: 1: 1) foll 4th row **and at same time** dec 1 st at neck edge on 4th and foll 4th (4th: 4th: 4th: 6th) row. 3 sts.
Work 5 (3: 3: 3: 3) rows, ending with a WS row.

Place marker at end of last row – this matches to fasten-off point of right back neck.
Cont as set on rem 3 sts for a further 9 (9: 9: 10: 10) cm for back neck border extension.
Cast off.
With RS facing, rejoin yarn to rem sts, K to end.
Working a slip st edging as described on the information page at neck edge (beg of RS rows and end of WS rows), cont as folls:
Work 2 rows.

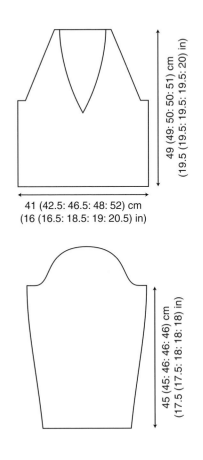

49 (49: 50: 50: 51) cm
(19.5 (19.5: 19.5: 19.5: 20) in)

41 (42.5: 46.5: 48: 52) cm
(16 (16.5: 18.5: 19: 20.5) in)

45 (45: 46: 46: 46) cm
(17.5 (17.5: 18: 18: 18) in)

Shape armhole

Cast off 2 sts at beg of next row.
9 (10: 11: 11: 12) sts.
Next row (RS): Patt 1 st, K2tog tbl, K to last 2 sts, K2tog. 7 (8: 9: 9: 10) sts.
Working all neck decreases as set by last row, complete to match first side, reversing shapings.

Cast on 25 (25: 25: 27: 27) sts using 9mm (US 13) needles and yarn A.
Work in moss st as given for back, shaping sides by inc 1 st at each end of 9th and every foll 6th row to 35 (35: 41: 35: 43) sts, then on every foll 8th row until there are 43 (43: 45: 45: 47) sts, taking inc sts into moss st.
Cont straight until sleeve measures 45 (45: 46: 46: 46) cm, ending with a WS row.

Shape top

Cast off 4 sts at beg of next 2 rows.
35 (35: 37: 37: 39) sts.
Dec 1 st at each end of next and every foll alt row to 23 sts, then on foll 7 rows, ending with a WS row. Cast off rem 9 sts.

PRESS as described on the information page. Join cast-off ends of back neck border extensions, then sew one edge to back neck, matching front markers to ends of back neck shaping.
See information page for finishing instructions, setting in sleeves using the set-in method.

No 12

MINGLE

ANNA WHEELER

Rowan Big Wool

A Cassis	024	2	x	100gm
B Pistachio	029	2	x	100gm
C Wild Berry	025	1	x	100gm
D Pip	015	1	x	100gm

1 pair 12mm (US 17) needles

9 sts and 9 rows to 10 cm measured over pattern using 12mm (US 17) needles.

Completed scarf measures 28 cm (11 in) wide and 201 cm (79 in) long.

Cast on 25 sts using 12mm (US 17) needles and yarn A.
Row 1 (WS): (P1, yrn, P7, yrn) 3 times, P1. 31 sts.
Row 2: (K1, K1 tbl, K2, sl 1, K2tog, psso, K2, K1 tbl) 3 times, K1. 25 sts.
These 2 rows form patt.
Joining in and breaking off colours as required, cont in patt as folls:
Using yarn A, work a further 9 rows, ending with a WS row.
Using yarn B, work 10 rows.
Using yarn C, work 10 rows.
Using yarn D, work 10 rows.
Using yarn A, work 10 rows.
Rep last 40 rows 3 times more.
Using yarn B, work 10 rows, ending with a WS row. Cast off in patt.

PRESS as described on the information page.

No 13

BISTO

MARTIN STOREY

YARN

	S	M	L	XL	XXL	
To fit chest	97	102	107	112	117	cm
	38	40	42	44	46	in

Rowan Big Wool

8 9 9 10 10 x 100gm

(photographed in Tremble 035)

NEEDLES

1 pair 10mm (no 000) (US 15) needles
1 pair 12mm (US 17) needles
Cable needle

TENSION

8 sts and 12 rows to 10 cm measured over stocking stitch using 12mm (US 17) needles.

SPECIAL ABBREVIATIONS

Cr3R = slip next st onto cable needle and leave at back of work, K2, then P1 from cable needle.

Cr3L = slip next 2 sts onto cable needle and leave at front of work, P1, then K2 from cable needle.

C4B = slip next 2 sts onto cable needle and leave at back of work, K2, then K2 from cable needle.

C4F = slip next 2 sts onto cable needle and leave at front of work, K2, then K2 from cable needle.

Make knot = (K next st and leaving original st on left needle and new loop on right needle, slip original loop to cable needle and leave at front of work) twice – 2 sts on cable needle. Join in new length of yarn and, beg with a K row, work in st st on the 2 sts on cable needle for 12 rows. Slip sts onto a safety pin and tie in a loose knot. On foll row, P tog each st from safety pin with corresponding st of main work.

BACK

Cast on 44 (46: 48: 50: 52) sts using 10mm (US 15) needles.

Row 1 (RS): P1 (0: 0: 0: 1), K2 (0: 1: 2: 2), *P2, K2, rep from * to last 1 (2: 3: 0: 1) sts, P1 (2: 2: 0: 1), K0 (0: 1: 0: 0).

Row 2: K1 (0: 0: 0: 1), P2 (0: 1: 2: 2), *K2, P2, rep from * to last 1 (2: 3: 0: 1) sts, K1 (2: 2: 0: 1), P0 (0: 1: 0: 0).

These 2 rows form rib.

Cont in rib for a further 8 rows, ending with a WS row.

Change to 12mm (US 17) needles.

Beg with a K row, cont in st st until back measures 43 cm, ending with a WS row.

Shape armholes

Cast off 3 sts at beg of next 2 rows. 38 (40: 42: 44: 46) sts.

Dec 1 st at each end of next 2 (2: 3: 3: 4) rows. 34 (36: 36: 38: 38) sts.

Cont straight until armhole measures 22 (23: 24: 25: 26) cm, ending with a WS row.

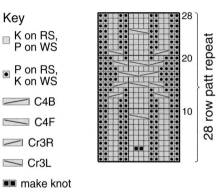

Key

▢ K on RS,
P on WS

▣ P on RS,
K on WS

▱ C4B

▱ C4F

▱ Cr3R

▱ Cr3L

■■ make knot

Shape shoulders and back neck

Next row (RS): Cast off 5 sts, K until there are 8 (9: 9: 9: 9) sts on right needle and turn, leaving rem sts on a holder.

Work each side of neck separately.

Cast off 3 sts at beg of next row.

Cast off rem 5 (6: 6: 6: 6) sts.

With RS facing, rejoin yarn to rem sts, cast off centre 8 (8: 8: 10: 10) sts, K to end.

Complete to match first side, reversing shapings.

FRONT

Cast on 46 (48: 50: 52: 54) sts using 10mm (US 15) needles.

Row 1 (RS): P1 (0: 0: 0: 1), K2 (0: 1: 2: 2), (P2, K2) 5 (6: 6: 6: 6) times, (K2, P2) 5 (6: 6: 6: 6) times, K2 (0: 1: 2: 2), P1 (0: 0: 0: 1).

Row 2: K1 (0: 0: 0: 1), P2 (0: 1: 2: 2), (K2, P2) 5 (6: 6: 6: 6) times, (P2, K2) 5 (6: 6: 6: 6) times, P2 (0: 1: 2: 2), K1 (0: 0: 0: 1).

These 2 rows form rib.

Cont in rib for a further 4 rows, ending with a WS row.

Row 7 (RS): Rib 21 (22: 23: 24: 25), C4F, rib to end.

Work in rib for a further 3 rows, ending with a WS row.

Change to 12mm (US 17) needles.

Row 1 (RS): K15 (16: 17: 18: 19), work next 16 sts as row 1 of chart for cable panel, K to end.

Row 2: P15 (16: 17: 18: 19), work next 16 sts as row 2 of chart for cable panel, P to end.

These 2 rows set the sts – central cable panel with sts either side in st st.

Cont as set until front matches back to beg of armhole shaping, ending with a WS row.

Shape armholes

Keeping patt correct, cast off 3 sts at beg of next 2 rows. 40 (42: 44: 46: 48) sts.

Dec 1 st at each end of next 2 (2: 3: 3: 4) rows. 36 (38: 38: 40: 40) sts.

Cont straight until 6 rows less have been worked than on back to start of shoulder shaping, ending with a WS row.

Shape neck

Next row (RS): Patt 14 (15: 15: 15: 15) sts and turn, leaving rem sts on a holder.

Work each side of neck separately.

Dec 1 st at neck edge of next 3 rows, then on foll alt row, ending with a WS row. 10 (11: 11: 11: 11) sts.

Shape shoulder

Cast off 5 sts at beg of next row.

Work 1 row.

Cast off rem 5 (6: 6: 6: 6) sts.

With RS facing, rejoin yarn to rem sts, cast off centre 8 (8: 8: 10: 10) sts, patt to end.

Complete to match first side, reversing shapings.

SLEEVES (both alike)

Cast on 24 (24: 24: 26: 26) sts using 10mm (US 15) needles.

Row 1 (RS): K0 (0: 0: 1: 1), (P2, K2) 3 times, (K2, P2) 3 times, K0 (0: 0: 1: 1).

Row 2: P0 (0: 0: 1: 1), (K2, P2) 3 times, (P2, K2) 3 times, P0 (0: 0: 1: 1).

These 2 rows form rib.

Cont in rib for a further 4 rows, ending with a WS row.

Row 7 (RS): Rib 10 (10: 10: 11: 11), C4F, rib to end.

Work in rib for a further 3 rows, ending with a WS row.

Change to 12mm (US 17) needles.

Row 1 (RS): Inc in first st, K3 (3: 3: 4: 4), work next 16 sts as row 1 of chart for cable panel, K to last st, inc in last st. 26 (26: 26: 28: 28) sts.

Row 2: P5 (5: 5: 6: 6), work next 16 sts as row 2 of chart for cable panel, P to end.

These 2 rows set the sts – central cable panel with sts either side in st st.

Cont as now set, shaping sides by inc 1 st at each end of 7th (7th: 5th: 7th: 5th) and every foll 8th (8th: 6th: 8th: 8th) row to 34 (32: 30: 32: 40) sts, then on every foll 10th (10th: 8th: 10th: -) row until there are 36 (36: 38: 38: -) sts, taking inc sts into st st.

Cont straight until sleeve measures 49 (50: 50: 51: 51) cm, ending with a WS row.

Shape top

Keeping patt correct, cast off 3 sts at beg of next 2 rows. 30 (30: 32: 32: 34) sts.

Dec 1 st at each end of next and every foll 4th row to 24 (24: 26: 26: 28) sts then on every foll alt row to 18 sts, then on foll 3 rows, ending with a WS row.

Cast off rem 12 sts.

MAKING UP

PRESS as described on the information page. Join right shoulder seam using back stitch, or mattress stitch if preferred.

Collar

With RS facing and using 10mm (US 15) needles, pick up and knit 8 sts down left side of neck, 8 (8: 8: 10: 10) sts from front, 8 sts up right side of neck, then 14 (14: 14: 16: 16) sts from back. 38 (38: 38: 42: 42) sts.

Row 1 (WS): P2, ★K2, P2, rep from ★ to end.

Row 2: K2, ★P2, K2, rep from ★ to end.

These 2 rows form rib.

Cont in rib until collar measures 9 cm.

Change to 12mm (US 17) needles.

Cont in rib until collar measures 18 cm.

Cast off in rib.

See information page for finishing instructions, setting in sleeves using the set-in method and reversing collar seam for turn-back.

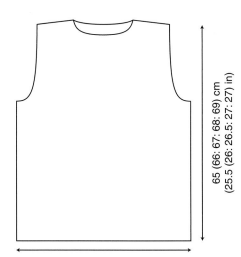

55 (57.5: 60: 62.5: 65) cm
(21.5 (22.5: 23.5: 24.5: 25.5) in)

65 (66: 67: 68: 69) cm
(25.5 (26: 26.5: 27: 27) in)

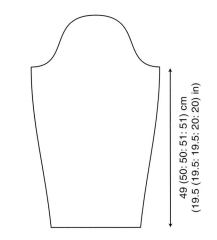

49 (50: 50: 51: 51) cm
(19.5 (19.5: 19.5: 20: 20) in)

YARN

	ladies			mens		
	S	M	L	M	L	XL
To fit bust/	86	91	97	102	107	112	cm
chest	34	36	38	40	42	44	in

Rowan Biggy Print and Big Wool
A Biggy Print 9 10 11 12 13 14 x 100gm
B Big Wool 2 2 3 3 3 3 x 100gm
(ladies photographed in Thunder 252 trimmed with Smoky 007, mans in Humbug 254 trimmed with Smoky 007)

NEEDLES

1 pair 10mm (no 000) (US 15) needles
1 pair 15mm (US 19) needles
1 pair 20mm (US 36) needles

BUTTONS

9 (**11**) x 00326

TENSION

5½ sts and 7 rows to 10 cm measured over stocking stitch using 20mm (US 36) needles and Biggy Print.

Pattern note: The pattern is written for the 3 ladies sizes, followed by the mens sizes in **bold**. Where only one figure appears this applies to all sizes in that group.

BACK

Cast on 23 (25: 27: **29: 31: 33**) sts using 20mm (US 36) needles and yarn A.
Beg with a K row, cont in st st, shaping side seams by inc 1 st at each end of 5th (**9th**) and foll 8th row. 27 (29: 31: **33: 35: 37**) sts.
Cont straight until back measures 28 (29: 30: **33: 34: 35**) cm, ending with a WS row.

Shape armholes

Cast off 2 sts at beg of next 2 rows.
23 (25: 27: **29: 31: 33**) sts.
Dec 1 st at each end of next 2 rows.
19 (21: 23: **25: 27: 29**) sts.
Cont straight until armhole measures 20 (21: 22: **23: 24: 25**) cm, ending with a WS row.

Shape shoulders

Cast off 2 (3: 3: **3: 4: 4**) sts at beg of next 2 rows, then 3 (3: 4: **4: 4: 5**) sts at beg of foll 2 rows.
Cast off rem 9 (**11**) sts.

LEFT FRONT

Cast on 12 (13: 14: **15: 16: 17**) sts using 20mm (US 36) needles and yarn A.
Beg with a K row, cont in st st, shaping side seam by inc 1 st at beg of 5th (**9th**) and foll 8th row. 14 (15: 16: **17: 18: 19**) sts.
Cont straight until left front matches back to beg of armhole shaping, ending with a WS row.

Shape armhole

Cast off 2 sts at beg of next row.
12 (13: 14: **15: 16: 17**) sts.
Work 1 row.
Dec 1 st at armhole edge of next 2 rows.
10 (11: 12: **13: 14: 15**) sts.
Cont straight until 3 rows less have been worked than on back to start of shoulder shaping, ending with a RS row.

Shape neck

Cast off 3 (**4**) sts at beg of next row.
7 (8: 9: **9: 10: 11**) sts.
Dec 1 st at neck edge of next 2 rows, ending with a WS row. 5 (6: 7: **7: 8: 9**) sts.

Shape shoulder

Cast off 2 (3: 3: **3: 4: 4**) sts at beg of next row.
Work 1 row.
Cast off rem 3 (3: 4: **4: 4: 5**) sts.

RIGHT FRONT

Cast on 12 (13: 14: **15: 16: 17**) sts using 20mm (US 36) needles and yarn A.
Beg with a K row, cont in st st, shaping side seam by inc 1 st at end of 5th (**9th**) and foll 8th row. 14 (15: 16: **17: 18: 19**) sts.
Complete to match left front, reversing shapings.

SLEEVES (both alike)

Cast on 14 (**16**) sts using 20mm (US 36) needles and yarn A.
Beg with a K row, cont in st st, shaping sides by inc 1 st at each end of 3rd (**7th**) and every foll 8th (6th: 6th: **6th: 6th: 4th**) row until there are 20 (22: 22: **24: 24: 26**) sts.
Cont straight until sleeve measures 40 (41: 42: **43: 44: 45**) cm, ending with a WS row.

Shape top

Cast off 2 sts at beg of next 2 rows.
16 (18: 18: **20: 20: 22**) sts.
Dec 1 st at each end of next and every foll alt row to 8 (**12**) sts, then on foll 1 (**3**) rows, ending with a WS row.
Cast off rem 6 sts.

MAKING UP

PRESS as described on the information page. Join both shoulder seams using back stitch, or mattress stitch if preferred.

Collar

With RS facing, using 15mm (US 19) needles and yarn B (**A**), starting and ending at front opening edges, pick up and knit 9 sts up right side of neck, 9 (**11**) sts from back, then 9 sts down left side of neck. 27 (**29**) sts.
Row 1 (WS): P1, ★K1, P1, rep from ★ to end.

Row 2: K1, ★P1, K1, rep from ★ to end.
Rep last 2 rows until collar measures 12 cm.
Cast off in rib.

Button band
Cast on 5 sts using 10mm (US 15) needles and yarn B.
Row 1 (RS): K2, P1, K2.
Row 2: K1, (P1, K1) twice.
These 2 rows form rib.
Cont in rib until button band, when slightly stretched, fits up entire left (**right**) front opening edge, from cast-on edge to cast-off edge of collar.
Cast off.
Slip stitch band in place.
Mark positions for 6 buttons on this band – first to come 3 cm up from lower edge, last to come 3 cm down from top of collar and rem 4 buttons evenly spaced between.

Buttonhole band
Cast on 5 sts using 10mm (US 15) needles and yarn B.
Cont in rib as given for button band until buttonhole band, when slightly stretched, fits up entire right (**left**) front opening edge, from cast-on edge to cast-off edge of collar, with

the addition of 6 buttonholes worked to correspond with positions marked for buttons on button band as folls:
Buttonhole row (RS): K1, P1, yrn, P2tog, K1.
When band is complete, cast off.
Slip stitch band in place.
See information page for finishing instructions, setting in sleeves using the set-in method.

Waistband
Cast on 7 sts using 10mm (US 15) needles and yarn B.
Row 1 (RS): K2, P1, K1, P1, K2.
Row 2: K1, (P1, K1) 3 times.
These 2 rows form rib.
Cont in rib until waistband, when slightly stretched, fits along lower edge from front opening edge of button band to centre of buttonhole band, ending with a WS row.
Next row (buttonhole row) (RS): K2, P1, yrn, P2tog, K2.
Work 5 rows.
Rep buttonhole row once more.
Work 3 rows, ending with a WS row.
Next row (RS): K2, sl 1, K2tog, psso, K2.
5 sts.

Next row: K1, P3tog, K1.
Next row: sl 1, K2tog, psso and fasten off.
Slip st waistband in place, leaving last section free to form overlap.

Cuffs (make 2)
Cast on 7 sts using 10mm (US 15) needles and yarn B.
Work in rib as given for waistband until cuff, when slightly stretched, fits along lower edge of sleeve, ending with a WS row.

Mens sizes only
Next row (buttonhole row) (RS): K2, P1, yrn, P2tog, K2.
Work 5 rows.

All sizes
Next row (buttonhole row) (RS): K2, P1, yrn, P2tog, K2.
Work 3 rows, ending with a WS row.
Next row (RS): K2, sl 1, K2tog, psso, K2.
5 sts.
Next row: K1, P3tog, K1.
Next row: sl 1, K2tog, psso and fasten off.
Overlap ends of cuffs so that pointed end is uppermost and then slip st to cast-on edge of sleeves, positioning cuff so that point is level with sleeve seam. Sew on buttons.

53 (55: 57: **61: 63: 65**) cm
(21 (21.5: 22.5: **24: 25: 25.5**) in)

49 (52.5: 56.5: **60: 63.5: 67.5**) cm
(19.5 (20.5: 22: **23.5: 25: 26.5**) in)

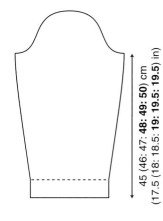

45 (46: 47: **48: 49: 50**) cm
(17.5 (18: 18.5: **19: 19.5: 19.5**) in)

No 15

COTY

KIM HARGREAVES

YARN

	XS-M	M-XL	
To fit bust	81-91	91-102	cm
	32-36	36-40	in

Rowan Chunky Print

3   4   x   100gm

(photographed in Tart 074)

CROCHET HOOK

9.00mm (no 00) crochet hook
.

TENSION

2½ pattern repeats and 5 rows to 10 cm measured over pattern using 9.00mm crochet hook.

CROCHET ABBREVIATIONS

ch = chain; **ss** = slip stitch;
dc = double crochet; **tr** = treble;
dtr = double treble; **sp(s)** = space(s).

PONCHO (worked downwards)

Using 9.00mm hook, make 64 (72) ch and join with a ss to form a ring.

Round 1: (5 ch, miss 3 ch, 1 dc into next ch) 7 (8) times, 5 ch, miss 3 ch, (1 dc, 5 ch and 1 ss) into next ch, (5 ch, miss 3 ch, 1 dc into next ch) 7 (8) times, 5 ch, miss 3 ch, (1 dc, 3 ch and 1 dtr) into next ch.
18 (20) ch sps.

Round 2: (5 ch, 1 dc into next ch sp) 17 (19) times, 5 ch, ss to top of dtr at end of previous round.

Round 3: (5 ch, 1 dc into next ch sp) 9 (10) times, 5 ch, (1 dc, 5 ch and 1 ss) into next dc, (5 ch, 1 dc into next ch sp) 9 (10) times, 5 ch, (1 ss, 3 ch and 1 dtr) into base of 5 ch at beg of round. 22 (24) ch sps.

Round 4: (5 ch, 1 dc into next ch sp) 21 (23) times, 5 ch, ss to top of dtr at end of previous round.

Round 5: (5 ch, 1 dc into next ch sp) 22 (24) times, 3 ch, ss to 3rd of 5 ch at beg of round.

Round 6: (5 ch, 1 dc into next ch sp) 10 (11) times, 5 ch, (1 dc, 5 ch and 1 ss) into next ch sp, (5 ch, 1 dc into next ch sp) 10 (11) times, 5 ch, (1 ss, 3 ch and 1 dtr) into ss at end of previous round. 24 (26) ch sps.

Round 7: (5 ch, 1 dc into next ch sp) 23 (25) times, 5 ch, ss to top of dtr at end of previous round.

Round 8: (5 ch, 1 dc into next ch sp) 24 (26) times, 3 ch, ss to 3rd of 5 ch at beg of round.

Round 9: (5 ch, 1 dc into next ch sp) 11 (12) times, 5 ch, (1 dc, 5 ch and 1 ss) into next ch sp, (5 ch, 1 dc into next ch sp) 11 (12) times, 5 ch, (1 ss, 3 ch and 1 dtr) into ss at end of previous round. 26 (28) ch sps.

Round 10: (5 ch, 1 dc into next ch sp) 25 (27) times, 5 ch, ss to top of dtr at end of previous round.

Round 11: (5 ch, 1 dc into next ch sp) 26 (28) times, 3 ch, ss to 3rd of 5 ch at beg of round.

Round 12: (5 ch, 1 dc into next ch sp) 12 (13) times, 5 ch, (1 dc, 5 ch and 1 ss) into next ch sp, (5 ch, 1 dc into next ch sp) 12 (13) times, 5 ch, (1 ss, 3 ch and 1 dtr) into ss at end of previous round. 28 (30) ch sps.

Round 13: (5 ch, 1 dc into next ch sp) 27 (29) times, 5 ch, ss to top of dtr at end of previous round.

Round 14: (5 ch, 1 dc into next ch sp) 28 (30) times, 3 ch, ss to 3rd of 5 ch at beg of round.

Round 15: (5 ch, 1 dc into next ch sp) 13 (14) times, 5 ch, (1 dc, 5 ch and 1 ss) into next ch sp, (5 ch, 1 dc into next ch sp) 13 (14) times, 5 ch, (1 ss, 5 ch and 1 dtr) into ss at end of previous round. 30 (32) ch sps.

Round 16: (5 ch, 1 dc into next ch sp) 29 (31) times, 5 ch, ss to top of dtr at end of previous round.

Round 17: 5 ch, 1 dc into next ch sp, ★5 tr into next dc, 1 dc into next ch sp★★, 5 ch, 1 dc into next ch sp, rep from ★ to end, ending last rep at ★★, 3 ch, ss to 3rd of 5 ch at beg of round.

Round 18: ★5 ch, 1 dc into 3rd tr of next group of 5 tr, 5 ch, 1 dc into next ch sp, rep from ★ to end, working last dc into ss at end of previous round.

Round 19: 3 ch (counts as first tr), 2 tr into dc at base of 3 ch, 1 dc into next ch sp, ★5 ch, 1 dc into next ch sp★★, 5 tr into next dc, 1 dc

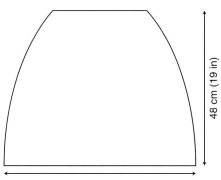

64 (68) cm (25 (27) in)

48 cm (19 in)

into next ch sp, rep from ★ to end, ending last rep at ★★, 2 tr into dc at base of 3 ch at beg of round, ss to top of 3 ch at beg of round.
Round 20: (5 ch, miss 5 sts, 1 dc into next st) 14 (15) times, 5 ch, miss 5 sts, (1 dc, 5 ch and 1 ss) into next st, (5 ch, miss 5 sts, 1 dc into next st) 14 (15) times, 5 ch, miss 5 sts, (1 ss, 3 ch and 1 dtr) into ss at end of previous round. 32 (34) ch sps.

Round 21: (5 ch, 1 dc into next ch sp) 31 (33) times, 5 ch, ss to top of dtr at end of previous round.
Round 22: (5 ch, 1 dc into next ch sp) 32 (34) times, 3 ch, ss to 3rd of 5 ch at beg of round.
Round 23: (5 ch, 1 dc into next ch sp) 31 (33) times, 5 ch, ss to base of 5 ch at beg of round.

Round 24: 3 ch (counts as first tr), 2 tr into ss at base of 3 ch, 1 dc into next ch sp, ★5 tr into next dc, 1 dc into next ch sp, rep from ★ to end, 2 tr into ss at base of 3 ch at beg of round, ss to top of 3 ch at beg of round. Fasten off.

MAKING UP
PRESS as described on the information page.

No 16

ONA

KIM HARGREAVES

YARN
One size
Rowan Big Wool
   1   x   100gm
(photographed in Smooch 031)

NEEDLES
1 pair 10mm (no 000) (US 15) needles
1 pair 12mm (US 17) needles

TENSION
8 sts and 12 rows to 10 cm measured over stocking stitch using 12mm (US 17) needles.

HAT
Cast on 37 sts using 10mm (US 15) needles. Beg with a P row, work in rev st st for 2 rows, ending with a WS row.
Change to 12mm (US 17) needles.
Work in rev st st for a further 14 rows, ending with a WS row.
Shape top
Row 1 (RS): (P4, P2tog) 6 times, P1. 31 sts.
Work 3 rows.
Row 5: (P3, P2tog) 6 times, P1. 25 sts.
Work 1 row.
Row 7: (P2, P2tog) 6 times, P1. 19 sts.

Work 1 row.
Row 9: (P1, P2tog) 6 times, P1. 13 sts.
Row 10: (K2tog, K1) 4 times, K1. 9 sts.
Work 8 rows.
Change to 10mm (US 15) needles.
Work a further 6 rows, ending with a WS row. Break yarn and thread through rem 9 sts. Pull up tight and fasten off securely.

MAKING UP
PRESS as described on the information page. Join back seam. Make a 6 cm diameter pompom and attach to top of hat.

No 17

EMMA

LAURA LONG

YARN

	XS	S	M	L	XL	
To fit bust	81	86	91	97	102	cm
	32	34	36	38	40	in

Rowan Big Wool and Biggy Print

A Wool Sugar Spun 016

	8	8	9	9	10	x 100gm

B Print Glum 244

	2	2	2	2	3	x 100gm

NEEDLES

1 pair 10mm (no 000) (US 15) needles
1 pair 12mm (US 17) needles

TENSION

8 sts and 12 rows to 10 cm measured over
stocking stitch using 12mm (US 17) needles.

BACK

Cast on 40 (42: 44: 46: 48) sts using 10mm
(US 15) needles and yarn A.
Row 1 (RS): K1 (0: 0: 0: 1), P2 (0: 1: 2: 2),
★K2, P2, rep from ★ to last 1 (2: 3: 0: 1) sts,
K1 (2: 2: 0: 1), P0 (0: 1: 0: 0).
Row 2: P1 (0: 0: 0: 1), K2 (0: 1: 2: 2), ★P2, K2,
rep from ★ to last 1 (2: 3: 0: 1) sts, P1 (2: 2: 0: 1),
K0 (0: 1: 0: 0).
These 2 rows form rib.
Work in rib for a further 6 rows, ending with
a WS row.
Change to 12mm (US 17) needles.
Joining in and breaking off colours as
required, cont in patt as folls:
Row 1 (RS): Using yarn A, knit.
Row 2: Using yarn A, purl.
Row 3: As row 1.
Row 4: Using yarn B, knit.
These 4 rows form patt.

Work in patt for a further 16 rows, ending
with a WS row.
Break off yarn B and cont in st st, beg with a
K row, using yarn A only.
Cont straight until back measures 45 cm,
ending with a WS row.
Shape raglan armholes
Cast off 4 sts at beg of next 2 rows.
32 (34: 36: 38: 40) sts.
Dec 1 st at each end of next and every foll
4th row to 22 (26: 28: 30: 32) sts, then on every
foll alt row until 16 (16: 16: 18: 18) sts rem.
Work 1 row, ending with a WS row.
Cast off.

FRONT

Work as given for back until 24 (24: 24: 26:
26) sts rem in raglan armhole shaping.
Work 3 (1: 1: 1: 1) rows, ending with a WS
row.
Shape neck
Next row (RS): K2tog, K4 and turn, leaving
rem sts on a holder. 5 sts.
Work each side of neck separately.
Dec 1 st at neck edge of next 3 rows **and at
same time** dec 1 st at raglan armhole edge
on 2nd row, ending with a WS row.
Fasten off rem 1 st.
With RS facing, rejoin yarn to rem sts, cast off
centre 12 (12: 12: 14: 14) sts, K to last 2 sts,
K2tog.
Complete to match first side, reversing shapings.

SLEEVES

Cast on 24 (24: 24: 26: 26) sts using 10mm
(US 15) needles and yarn A.
Row 1 (RS): P1 (1: 1: 2: 2), ★K2, P2, rep from
★ to last 3 (3: 3: 4: 4) sts, K2, P1 (1: 1: 2: 2).

Row 2: K1 (1: 1: 2: 2), ★P2, K2, rep from ★ to
last 3 (3: 3: 4: 4) sts, P2, K1 (1: 1: 2: 2).
These 2 rows form rib.
Work in rib for a further 6 rows, ending with
a WS row.
Change to 12mm (US 17) needles.
Work in patt as given for back for 20 rows
and at same time inc 1 st at each end of 7th
and foll 0 (0: 10th: 0: 10th) row, ending with a
WS row.
26 (26: 28: 28: 30) sts.
Break off yarn B and cont in st st, beg with a
K row, using yarn A only.
Inc 1 st at each end of 3rd (3rd: 7th: 3rd: 7th)
and foll 16th (16th: 12th: 16th: 12th) row.
30 (30: 32: 32: 34) sts.
Cont straight until sleeve measures 43 (43: 44:
44: 44) cm, ending with a WS row.
Shape raglan
Cast off 4 sts at beg of next 2 rows.
22 (22: 24: 24: 26) sts.
Dec 1 st at each end of next and every foll alt
row to 12 sts, then on every foll 4th row until
6 sts rem, ending with a RS row.
Left sleeve only
Dec 1 st at beg of next row and at same edge
on foll 2 rows.
Right sleeve only
Dec 1 st at end of next row and at same edge
on foll 2 rows.
Both sleeves
Cast off rem 3 sts.

MAKING UP

PRESS as described on the information page.
Join both front and right back raglan seams
using back stitch, or mattress stitch if
preferred.

Collar

With RS facing, using 10mm (US 15) needles and yarn A, pick up and knit 5 sts from top of left sleeve, 3 sts down left side of neck, 12 (12: 12: 14: 14) sts from front, 3 sts up right side of neck, 5 sts from top of right sleeve, then 16 (16: 16: 18: 18) sts from back.

44 (44: 44: 48: 48) sts.

Beg with a K row, work in st st for 12 cm.

Change to 12mm (US 17) needles.

Cont in st st until collar measures 18 cm, ending with a P row.

Joining in and breaking off colours as required, cont in patt as folls:

Row 1 (RS of collar): Using yarn A, K4, *M1, K4, rep from * to end.

54 (54: 54: 59: 59) sts.

Row 2: Using yarn A, purl.

Row 3: Using yarn A, knit.

Row 4: Using yarn B, knit.

Row 5: As row 3.

Rows 6 to 9: As rows 2 to 5.

Row 10: As row 2.

Row 11: Using yarn A, K3 (3: 3: 2: 2), *M1, K3, rep from * to end.

71 (71: 71: 78: 78) sts.

Row 12: As row 4.

Row 13: As row 3.

Rows 14 to 17: As rows 2 to 5.

Rows 18 and 19: As rows 2 and 3.

Using yarn A, cast off knitwise (on WS).

See information page for finishing instructions, reversing collar seam for turn-back.

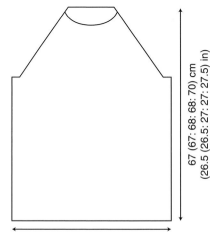

67 (67: 68: 68: 70) cm
(26.5 (26.5: 27: 27: 27.5) in)

50 (52.5: 55: 57.5: 60) cm
(19.5 (20.5: 21.5: 22.5: 23.5) in)

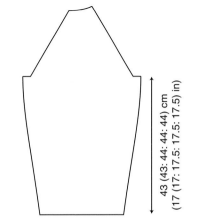

43 (43: 44: 44: 44) cm
(17 (17: 17.5: 17.5: 17.5) in)

BIDDY

KIM HARGREAVES

YARN

	XS	S	M	L	XL
To fit bust	81	86	91	97	102	cm
	32	34	36	38	40	in

Rowan Chunky Print

| | 3 | 3 | 4 | 4 | 5 x 100gm |

(photographed in Temper 073)

NEEDLES

1 pair 7mm (no 2) (US 10½) needles
1 pair 8mm (no 0) (US 11) needles

THONGING – 120 cm of leather thonging

TENSION

11 sts and 14 rows to 10 cm measured over stocking stitch using 8mm (US 11) needles.

FRONT
(knitted sideways from right side seam)

Cast on 33 (34: 34: 35: 35) sts using 8mm (US 11) needles.
Row 1 (RS): P2, K3, wrap next st (by slipping next st onto right needle, taking yarn to opposite side of work between needles and then slipping same st back onto left needle – when working back across sts, work the wrapped st and the loop tog as 1 st) and turn.
Row 2: Purl.
Row 3: P2, K7, wrap next st and turn.
Row 4: Purl.
Row 5: P2, K11, wrap next st and turn.
Row 6: Purl.
Row 7: P2, K to end.
Row 8: P7, wrap next st and turn.
Row 9: Knit.
Row 10: P11, wrap next st and turn.
Row 11: K to last st, inc in last st.

Row 12: Inc in first st, P15, wrap next st and turn.
Row 13: As row 11.
Row 14: Inc in first st, P to end. 37 (38: 38: 39: 39) sts.
This completes right side seam shaping.
Now working across all sts, cont as folls:
Row 15 (RS): P2, K to end.
Row 16: Cast on and P 17 (17: 18: 18: 19) sts, P to end. 54 (55: 56: 57: 58) sts.
Row 17: P2, K to last 2 sts, P2.
Row 18: Purl.★★
Rep rows 17 and 18, 7 (8: 9: 10: 11) times more.
Purl 10 rows, ending with a WS row.
Rep rows 17 and 18, 7 (8: 9: 10: 11) times more, then row 17 again, ending with a RS row.
★★★**Next row (WS):** Cast off 17 (17: 18: 18: 19) sts, P to end. 37 (38: 38: 39: 39) sts.
Next row: P2, K to last 2 sts, K2tog. 36 (37: 37: 38: 38) sts.
Shape left side seam
Row 1 (WS): P2tog, P16, wrap next st and turn.
Row 2: K to last 2 sts, K2tog.
Row 3: P2tog, P10, wrap next st and turn.
Row 4: Knit.
Row 5: P7, wrap next st and turn.
Row 6: Knit.
Row 7: Purl.
Row 8: P2, K11, wrap next st and turn.
Row 9: Purl.
Row 10: P2, K7, wrap next st and turn.
Row 11: Purl.
Row 12: P2, K3, wrap next st and turn.
Row 13: Purl.
Cast off all 33 (34: 34: 35: 35) sts.

LEFT BACK
(worked sideways from left side seam)

Work as given for front to ★★.
Rep rows 17 and 18, 5 (6: 7: 8: 9) times more, ending with a WS row.
Next row (RS): Purl.
Next row (eyelet row): P2, (P2tog, yrn, P6) 6 times, P2tog, yrn, P2 (3: 4: 5: 6).
Purl 3 rows, ending with a RS row.
Cast off knitwise (on WS).

RIGHT BACK
(worked sideways from centre back)

Cast on 54 (55: 56: 57: 58) sts using 8mm (US 11) needles.
Purl 3 rows, ending with a RS row.
Next row (eyelet row) (WS): P2, (P2tog, yrn, P6) 6 times, P2tog, yrn, P2 (3: 4: 5: 6).
Purl 2 rows, ending with a WS row.
Next row: P2, K to last 2 sts, P2.
Next row: Purl.

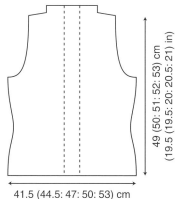

49 (50: 51: 52: 53) cm
(19.5 (19.5: 20: 20.5: 21) in)

41.5 (44.5: 47: 50: 53) cm
(16.5 (17.5: 18.5: 19.5: 21) in)

Rep last 2 rows 4 (5: 6: 7: 8) times more, then first of these 2 rows again, ending with a RS row. Complete as given for front from ★★★.

MAKING UP
PRESS as described on the information page.

Leaving 20 (20: 20: 21: 21) cm open at centre for neck, join both shoulder seams using back stitch, or mattress stitch if preferred.
Armhole borders (both alike)
With RS facing and using 7mm (US 10½) needles, pick up and knit 51 (51: 53: 53: 55) sts

all round armhole edge.
Work in garter st for 2 rows.
Cast off knitwise (on WS).
Join side and armhole border seams. Thread thonging in and out of eyelet holes to lace up back opening edge.

No 19

FOXY

CAROL MELDRUM

YARN
One size
Rowan Chunky Print and Big Wool
A Print Deep End 076   2   x   100gm
B Wool Ice Blue   021   1   x   100gm

NEEDLES
1 pair 7mm (no 2) (US 10½) needles

TENSION
9 sts and 13 rows to 10 cm measured over loop stitch pattern using 7mm (US 10½) needles and yarn A.

SPECIAL ABBREVIATION
Loop 1 = Insert right needle into next st as though to K this st, take yarn over needle and around first 2 fingers of left hand twice, then

around needle again, pull all 3 loops through st on left needle and place on left needle, leaving original st on left needle, then K tog tbl all 4 loops.

COLLAR
Cast on 3 sts using 7mm (US 10½) needles and yarn A.
Row 1 (RS): K3.
Row 2: K1, loop 1, K1.
Row 3: (K1, M1) twice, K1. 5 sts.
Row 4: K1, (loop 1, K1) twice.
Place marker on centre st of last row.
Row 5: K to marked st, M1, K marked st, M1, K to end.
Row 6: K1, ★loop 1, K1, rep from ★ to end.
Rep rows 5 and 6, 8 times more. 23 sts.
Row 23: Knit.

Row 24: K1, ★loop 1, K1, rep from ★ to end.
Rep last 2 rows until collar measures 30 cm from cast-on edge, ending with a WS row.
Next row (RS): K to within 2 sts of marked st, K2tog tbl, K marked st, K2tog, K to end.
Next row: K1, ★loop 1, K1, rep from ★ to end.
Rep last 2 rows until 3 sts rem.
Cast off.

MAKING UP
PRESS as described on the information page.
Using yarn A and yarn B, make two 9 cm diameter pompoms. Using yarn B, make two 25 cm long twisted cords.
Attach a pompom to one end of each cord, then attach other end of cord to ends of collar.

No 20

RENE

LEAH SUTTON

YARN

Rowan Big Wool

3 x 100gm

(photographed in Pip 015)

NEEDLES

1 pair 10mm (no 000) (US 15) needles

EXTRAS – 120 cm of 6 cm wide petersham ribbon

TENSION

12 sts and 12 rows to 10 cm measured over pattern using 10mm (US 15) needles.

FINISHED SIZE

Completed bag measures 27 cm (10½ in) in diameter.

SIDES (make 2)

Cast on 12 sts using 10mm (US 15) needles.

Row 1 (RS): Purl.

Row 2: Inc in first st, ★P3tog, (K1, P1, K1) all into next st, rep from ★ to last 3 sts, K2, inc in last st. 14 sts.

Row 3: Inc in first st, P to last st, inc in last st. 16 sts.

Row 4: Inc in first st, K2, ★(K1, P1, K1) all into next st, P3tog, rep from ★ to last st, inc in last st. 18 sts.

Row 5: As row 3. 20 sts.

Rows 6 to 9: As rows 2 to 5. 28 sts.

Rows 10 and 11: As rows 2 and 3. 32 sts.

Row 12: K3, ★(K1, P1, K1) all into next st, P3tog, rep from ★ to last st, K1.

Row 13: Purl.

Row 14: K3, ★P3tog, (K1, P1, K1) all into next st, rep from ★ to last st, K1.

Row 15: Purl.

Rows 16 to 19: As rows 12 to 15.

Rows 20 to 22: As rows 12 to 14.

Row 23: P2tog, P to last st, P2tog. 30 sts.

Row 24: K2tog, K2, ★(K1, P1, K1) all into next st, P3tog, rep from ★ to last 2 sts, K2tog. 28 sts.

Row 25: As row 23. 26 sts.

Row 26: K2tog, ★P3tog, (K1, P1, K1) all into next st, rep from ★ to last 4 sts, K2, K2tog. 24 sts.

Rows 27 to 30: As rows 23 to 26. 16 sts.

Place markers at both ends of last row.

Rows 31 and 32: As rows 23 and 24. 12 sts.

Row 33: Knit.

Cast off knitwise (on WS).

HANDLE AND GUSSET

Cast on 12 sts using 10mm (US 15) needles.

Row 1 (RS): K1, P10, K1.

Row 2: K2, ★P3tog, (K1, P1, K1) all into next st, rep from ★ once more, K2.

Row 3: As row 1.

Row 4: K2, ★(K1, P1, K1) all into next st, P3tog, rep from ★ once more, K2.

Rep last 4 rows until work measures 115 cm, ending with a WS row.

Cast off.

MAKING UP

PRESS as described on the information page. Join cast-on and cast-off ends of handle and gusset to form a loop. Lay petersham ribbon onto WS and stitch in place. Positioning gusset seam halfway across cast-on edges of sides, sew gusset to sides below markers (section left free forms handle).

YARN

ladies mans

Rowan Chunky Print

ladies   mans

A Rage   079   Pit   080   1   1 x 100gm

B Woolly 071   Native 072   1   1 x 100gm

CROCHET HOOK

9.00mm (no 00) crochet hook

BUTTONS

Ladies version only: 8 assorted buttons

TENSION

9 sts and 10 rows to 10 cm measured over pattern using 9.00mm crochet hook.

CROCHET ABBREVIATIONS

ch = chain; **ss** = slip stitch;
dc = double crochet.

HAT

Using 9.00mm hook and yarn A, make 4 ch and join with a ss to form a ring.

Round 1 (RS): 1 ch (does NOT count as st), 15 dc into ring, ss to first dc. 15 sts.

Now working into **back loops only** of sts, cont as folls:

Round 2: 1 ch (does NOT count as st), (1 dc into each of next 2 dc, 2 dc into next dc) 5 times, ss to first dc. 20 sts.

Join in yarn B.

Round 3: Using yarn B, 1 ch (does NOT count as st), (1 dc into each of next 3 dc, 2 dc into next dc) 5 times, ss to first dc. 25 sts.

Round 4: Using yarn A, 1 ch (does NOT count as st), (1 dc into each of next 4 dc, 2 dc into next dc) 5 times, ss to first dc. 30 sts.

Last 2 rounds form stripe sequence.

Keeping stripes correct throughout, cont as folls:

Ladies version only

Round 5: 1 ch (does NOT count as st), 1 dc into each dc to end, ss to first dc.

Both versions

Next round: 1 ch (does NOT count as st), (1 dc into each of next 5 dc, 2 dc into next dc) 5 times, ss to first dc. 35 sts.

Next round: 1 ch (does NOT count as st), 1 dc into each dc to end, ss to first dc.

Rep last round 1 (0) times more.

Next round: 1 ch (does NOT count as st), (1 dc into each of next 6 dc, 2 dc into next dc) 5 times, ss to first dc. 40 sts.

Mens version only

Next round: 1 ch (does NOT count as st), 1 dc into each dc to end, ss to first dc.

Rep last round once more.

Next round: 1 ch (does NOT count as st), (1 dc into each of next 7 dc, 2 dc into next dc) 5 times, ss to first dc. 45 sts.

Both versions

Next round: 1 ch (does NOT count as st), 1 dc into each dc to end, ss to first dc.

Rep last round 13 (12) times more.

Next round: Using yarn B and working sts under both loops of sts of previous round, 1 ch (does NOT count as st), 1 dc into each dc to end, ss to first dc.

Fasten off.

MAKING UP

PRESS as described on the information page. For ladies version only, attach buttons to front of hat using photograph as a guide.

CLICK–CLACK

ANNA WHEELER

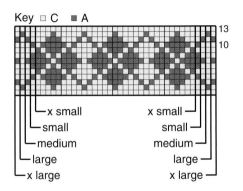

YARN

	XS	S	M	L	XL	
To fit bust	81	86	91	97	102	cm
	32	34	36	38	40	in

Rowan Big Wool

A Wild Berry	025	2	2	2	3	3 x 100gm
B Pip	015	1	1	2	2	2 x 100gm
C Pistachio	029	1	1	1	1	1 x 100gm

NEEDLES

1 pair 10mm (no 000) (US 15) needles
1 pair 12mm (US 17) needles

TENSION

8 sts and 12 rows to 10 cm measured over patterned stocking stitch using 12mm (US 17) needles.

BACK

Cast on 30 (32: 34: 36: 38) sts using 10mm (US 15) needles.
Row 1 (RS): K0 (0: 0: 1: 0), P0 (1: 2: 2: 0), ★K2, P2, rep from ★ to last 2 (3: 0: 1: 2) sts, K2 (2: 0: 1: 2), P0 (1: 0: 0: 0).
Row 2: P0 (0: 0: 1: 0), K0 (1: 2: 2: 0), ★P2, K2, rep from ★ to last 2 (3: 0: 1: 2) sts, P2 (2: 0: 1: 2), K0 (1: 0: 0: 0).
These 2 rows form rib.
Cont in rib for a further 5 rows, inc 1 st at end of last row and ending with a RS row.
31 (33: 35: 37: 39) sts.
Change to 12mm (US 17) needles.
Beg with a P row, cont in st st as folls:
Work 1 row.
Join in yarn B.
Using yarn B, work 2 rows.
Using yarn A, work 2 rows, ending with a WS row.

Starting and ending rows as indicated, using the **fairisle** technique as described on the information page, work in patt from chart, which is worked entirely in st st beg with a K row, for 13 rows, ending with a RS row.
Using yarn A, work 2 rows.
Using yarn B, work 2 rows.
Last 4 rows form striped st st.
Cont in striped st st until back measures 32 (33: 33: 34: 34) cm, ending with a WS row.
Shape armholes
Keeping stripes correct, cast off 2 sts at beg of next 2 rows. 27 (29: 31: 33: 35) sts.★★
Working a slip st edging as described on the information page at both ends of rows, cont as folls:
Next row (RS): Patt 1 st, K2tog tbl, K to last 3 sts, K2tog, patt 1 st.
Next row: Patt 1 st, P2tog, P to last 3 sts, P2tog tbl, patt 1 st.
These 2 rows set armhole decreases.
Working all armhole decreases as set by last 2 rows, dec 1 st at each end of next 0 (1: 1: 2: 2) rows. 23 (23: 25: 25: 27) sts.
Cont straight until armhole measures 19 (19: 20: 20: 21) cm, ending with a WS row.
Shape shoulders and back neck
Next row (RS): Cast off 3 sts, K until there are 5 (5: 6: 5: 6) sts on right needle and turn, leaving rem sts on a holder.
Work each side of neck separately.
Cast off 2 sts at beg of next row.
Cast off rem 3 (3: 4: 3: 4) sts.
With RS facing, rejoin appropriate yarn to rem sts, cast off centre 7 (7: 7: 9: 9) sts, patt to end.
Complete to match first side, reversing shapings.

FRONT

Work as given for back to ★★.
Working a slip st edging as described on the information page at both ends of rows, cont as folls:
Divide for neck
Next row (RS): Patt 1 st, K2tog tbl, K9 (10: 11: 12: 13), patt 1 st and turn, leaving rem sts on a holder. 12 (13: 14: 15: 16) sts.

51 (52: 53: 54: 55) cm
(20 (20.5: 21 21.5: 21.5) in)

39 (41.5: 44: 46.5: 49) cm
(15.5 (16.5: 17.5: 18.5: 19.5) in)

Key ☐ C ■ A

13
10

x small   x small
small   small
medium   medium
large   large
x large   x large

Work each side of neck separately.
Working all neck and armhole decreases in same way as back armhole decreases, dec 1 st at armhole edge of next 1 (2: 2: 3: 3) rows **and at same time** dec 1 st at neck edge on 0 (2nd: 2nd: 2nd: 2nd) row.
11 (10: 11: 11: 12) sts.
Dec 1 st at neck edge **only** on next (2nd: 4th: next: next) and foll 1 (0: 0: 1: 0) alt rows, then on every foll 4th row until 6 (6: 7: 6: 7) sts rem.
Cont straight until front matches back to start of shoulder shaping, ending with a WS row.

Shape shoulder
Cast off 3 sts at beg of next row.
Work 1 row.
Cast off rem 3 (3: 4: 3: 4) sts.
With RS facing, rejoin appropriate yarn to rem sts, K2tog, K to last 3 sts, K2tog, patt 1 st.
12 (13: 14: 15: 16) sts.
Complete to match first side, reversing shapings.

PRESS as described on the information page.
Join both shoulder seams using back stitch, or mattress stitch if preferred.
See information page for finishing instructions.

No 23

VINSTER

CAROL MELDRUM

YARN
One size
Rowan Big Wool
    1   x   100gm
(photographed in Cloak 034)

NEEDLES
1 pair 10mm (no 000) (US 15) needles

TENSION
9 sts and 15 rows to 10 cm measured over rib using 10mm (US 15) needles.

HAT
Cast on 42 sts using 10mm (US 15) needles.

Row 1 (RS): K2, ★P2, K2, rep from ★ to end.
Row 2: P2, ★K2, P2, rep from ★ to end.
These 2 rows form rib.
Cont in rib until hat measures 19 cm, ending with a RS row.
Next row (WS): P2, ★K2tog, P2, rep from ★ to end. 32 sts.
Next row: K2, ★P1, K2, rep from ★ to end.
Next row: P2, ★K1, P2, rep from ★ to end.
Rep last 2 rows twice more, ending with a WS row.
Next row (RS): Knit.
Next row: P16, fold work so that right sides are together and, using a spare needle, cast off both sets of sts together to form top seam.

MAKING UP
PRESS as described on the information page.
Join side seam, reversing seam for turn-back.
Make two 9 cm long tassels and two 6 cm long twisted or crochet cords.
Attach a tassel to one end of one cord and attach other end of cord to corner of top seam.
Attach other tassel and cord to other corner of top seam in same way.
Tie cords together to pull top of hat in to form a point.

No 24

MEGAN

LAURA LONG

YARN

	XS-S	S-M	M-L	L-XL	
To fit bust	81-86	86-91	91-97	97-102	cm
	32-34	34-36	36-38	38-40	in

Rowan Biggy Print

	5	5	6	7 x 100gm

(photographed in Razzle Dazzle 246)

NEEDLES

1 pair 20mm (US 36) needles

TENSION

5½ sts and 7 rows to 10 cm measured over stocking stitch using 20mm (US 36) needles.

PONCHO (worked in one piece)

Cast on 61 (65: 69: 73) sts using 20mm (US 36) needles.

Rows 1 to 3: Knit.

Row 4 (WS): P1, *yrn, P2tog, rep from * to end.

Rows 5 to 12: As rows 1 to 4, twice.

Rows 13 and 14: Knit.

Beg with a K row, cont in st st until work measures 25 cm, ending with a WS row.

Shape shoulders

Counting in from both ends of last row, place markers on 16th (17th: 18th: 19th) st in from both ends of row.

Row 1 (RS): *K to within 4 sts of marked st, K2tog tbl, K5 (marked st in centre st of this group of 5 sts), K2tog, rep from * once more, K to end. 57 (61: 65: 69) sts.

Work 3 (3: 1: 1) rows.

Next row: As row 1. 53 (57: 61: 65) sts.

Work 1 row.

Rep last 2 rows 2 (3: 4: 5) times more. 45 sts.

Cast off.

MAKING UP

PRESS as described on the information page. Join back seam using back stitch, or mattress stitch if preferred.

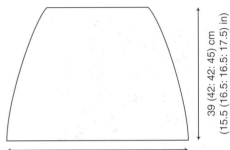

39 (42: 42: 45) cm
(15.5 (16.5: 16.5: 17.5) in)

55.5 (59: 62.5: 66.5) cm
(22 (23.5: 24.5: 26) in)

No 25

WANDA

KIM HARGREAVES

YARN

	XS	S	M	L	XL	
To fit bust	81	86	91	97	102	cm
	32	34	36	38	40	in

Rowan Chunky Print

| | 2 | 2 | 2 | 3 | 3 | x 100gm |

(photographed in Rage 079)

CROCHET HOOK

6.00mm (no 4) (US J10) crochet hook

RIBBON

150 cm of 3.5 cm wide satin ribbon

TENSION

12½ sts and 13 rows to 10 cm measured over pattern (double crochet fabric) using 6.00mm (US J10) crochet hook.

CROCHET ABBREVIATIONS

ch = chain;
ss = slip stitch;
dc = double crochet.

CORSET

Using 6.00mm (US J10) hook, make 20 ch.
Row 1: 1 dc into 2nd ch from hook, 1 dc into each ch to end, turn. 19 sts.
Row 2: 1 ch (does NOT count as st), 1 dc into each dc to end, turn.
Last row forms patt.
Cont in patt until work measures 12.5 (13.5: 15: 16: 17.5) cm.
★★Place marker at centre of last row.
Shape side
Row 1: 1 ch (does NOT count as st), 1 dc into each of first 7 dc, ss into next dc and turn, leaving rem 11 sts unworked.
Row 2: Ss into ss at end of previous row, 1 dc into each dc to end, turn.
Row 3: 1 ch (does NOT count as st), 1 dc into each of first 4 dc, ss into next dc and turn, leaving rem 14 sts unworked.
Row 4: Ss into ss at end of previous row, 1 dc into each dc to end, turn.
Row 5: 1 ch (does NOT count as st), 1 dc into each st to end, turn. 19 sts.

Rows 6 and 7: As rows 3 and 4.
Rows 8 and 9: As rows 1 and 2.
Row 10: As row 5. 19 sts.★★
Cont straight until work measures 30.5 (33: 35.5: 38: 40.5) cm from marker.
Rep from ★★ to ★★ once more.
Cont straight until work measures 12.5 (13.5: 15: 16: 17.5) cm from second marker.
Fasten off.

MAKING UP

PRESS as described on the information page.
Carefully pushing ribbon through crochet, thread ribbon in and out between sts to lace up front edges as in photograph.

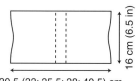

30.5 (33: 35.5: 38: 40.5) cm
(12 (13: 14: 15: 16) in)

16 cm (6.5 in)

No 26

BLOSSOM

KIM HARGREAVES

YARN

	XS-S	S-M	M-L	L-XL	
To fit bust	81-86	86-91	91-97	97-102	cm
	32-34	34-36	36-38	38-40	in

Rowan Biggy Print

| | 10 | 11 | 12 | 13 x 100gm |

(photographed in Giddy 239)

NEEDLES

1 pair 15mm (US 19) needles
1 pair 20mm (US 36) needles

BUTTONS – 1 x 00357

TENSION

5½ sts and 8 rows to 10 cm measured over
moss stitch using 20mm (US 36) needles.

BACK

Cast on 25 (27: 31: 33) sts using 20mm (US 36)
needles.
Row 1 (RS): P1, *K1, P1, rep from * to end.
Row 2: As row 1.
These 2 rows form moss st.
Cont in moss st until back measures 30 cm,
ending with a WS row.
Shape armholes
Keeping moss st correct, cast off 2 sts at beg of
next 2 rows. 21 (23: 27: 29) sts.
Dec 1 st at each end of next 1 (2: 3: 4) rows.
19 (19: 21: 21) sts.
Cont straight until armhole measures 19 (20:
21: 22) cm, ending with a WS row.
Shape shoulders and back neck
Next row (RS): Cast off 2 sts, moss st until
there are 5 sts on right needle and turn,
leaving rem sts on a holder.
Work each side of neck separately.

Cast off 2 sts at beg of next row.
Cast off rem 3 sts.
With RS facing, rejoin yarn to rem sts, cast off
centre 5 (5. 7. 7) sts, moss st to end.
Complete to match first side, reversing shapings.

LEFT FRONT

Cast on 13 (14: 16: 17) sts using 20mm (US 36)
needles.
Row 1 (RS): *P1, K1, rep from * to last 1 (0:
0: 1) st, P1 (0: 0: 1).
Row 2: P1 (0: 0: 1), *K1, P1, rep from * to end.
These 2 rows form moss st.
Cont in moss st until left front matches back
to beg of armhole shaping, ending with a WS
row.
Shape armhole
Keeping moss st correct, cast off 2 sts at beg of
next row. 11 (12: 14: 15) sts.
Work 1 row.
Dec 1 st at armhole edge of next 1 (2: 3: 4) rows.
10 (10: 11: 11) sts.
Cont straight until 5 rows less have been
worked than on back to start of shoulder
shaping, ending with a RS row.
Shape neck
Keeping moss st correct, cast off 3 (3: 4: 4) sts
at beg of next row. 7 sts.
Dec 1 st at neck edge of next 2 rows. 5 sts.
Work 2 rows, ending with a WS row
Shape shoulder
Cast off 2 sts at beg of next row.
Work 1 row.
Cast off rem 3 sts.

RIGHT FRONT

Cast on 13 (14: 16: 17) sts using 20mm (US 36)
needles.

Row 1 (RS): P1 (0: 0: 1), *K1, P1, rep from
* to end.
Row 2: *P1, K1, rep from * to last 1 (0: 0: 1) st,
P1 (0. 0. 1).
These 2 rows form moss st.
Complete to match left front, reversing shapings.

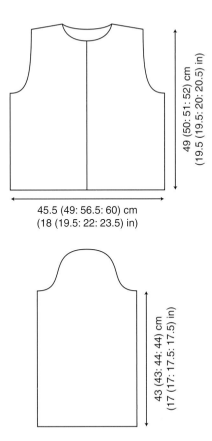

49 (50: 51: 52) cm
(19.5 (19.5: 20: 20.5) in)

45.5 (49: 56.5: 60) cm
(18 (19.5: 22: 23.5) in)

43 (43: 44: 44) cm
(17 (17: 17.5: 17.5) in)

Cast on 19 (19: 21: 21) sts using 20mm (US 36) needles.

Work in moss st as given for back until sleeve measures 43 (43: 44: 44) cm, ending with a WS row.

Shape top

Keeping moss st correct, cast off 2 sts at beg of next 2 rows. 15 (15: 17: 17) sts.

Dec 1 st at each end of next and foll 4th row, then on every foll alt row to 7 sts, then on foll row, ending with a WS row. Cast off rem 5 sts.

MAKING UP

PRESS as described on the information page. Join both shoulder seams using back stitch, or mattress stitch if preferred.

Neckband

With RS facing and using 15mm (US 19) needles, starting and ending at front opening edges, pick up and knit 9 (9: 10: 10) sts up right side of neck, 11 (11: 13: 13) sts from back, then 9 (9: 10: 10) sts down left side of neck. 29 (29: 33: 33) sts.

Cast off knitwise (on WS).

See information page for finishing instructions, setting in sleeves using the set-in method. Attach button to left front neck edge, easing it through sts of knitting of right front to form buttonhole.

No 27

BEAU

KIM HARGREAVES

YARN

One size

Rowan Biggy Print

2 x 100gm

(photographed in Splash 248)

or

Rowan Big Wool Tuft

3 x 50gm

(photographed in Shiver 056)

NEEDLES

1 pair 20mm (US 36) needles

FASTENER

1 large button or decorative brooch

TENSION

5½ sts and 8 rows to 10 cm measured over stocking stitch using 20mm (US 36) needles.

FINISHED SIZE

Completed collar is 18cm (7in) long and measures 91cm (36 in) around lower edge.

COLLAR

Cast on 50 sts loosely using 20mm (US 36) needles, taking time to pull "tufts" of yarn through sts if using Big Wool Tuft.

Beg with a K row, cont in st st as folls:

Work 2 rows.

Counting in from both ends of last row, place markers on 13th st in from both ends of last row.

Row 3 (dec): (K to within 2 sts of marked st, K2tog tbl, K marked st, K2tog) twice, K to end. 46 sts.

Work 3 rows.

Row 7: As row 3. 42 sts.

Work 3 rows.

Row 11: As row 3. 38 sts.

Work 1 row.

Row 13: As row 3. 34 sts.

Row 14: P5, P2tog tbl, P3, (P2tog) 3 times, P2, (P2tog tbl) 3 times, P3, P2tog, P to end. Cast off rem 26 sts.

MAKING UP

PRESS as described on the information page. If desired, attach button at neck edge, easing sts apart to form buttonhole at other end of neck edge.

RILLA

KIM HARGREAVES

YARN

Rowan Chunky Print

4   x   100gm

(photographed in Girly Pink 077)

CROCHET HOOK

9.00mm (no 00) crochet hook

FINISHED SIZE

Completed scarf measures approx 230 cm

(90½ in) long, and each length is approx 2.5 cm (1 in) wide.

CROCHET ABBREVIATIONS

ch = chain;
dc = double crochet.

SCARF

★Using 9.00mm hook, make a ch approx 230 cm long.

Row 1 (RS): 4 dc into 2nd ch from hook, 4 dc into each ch to end.
Fasten off.★
Rep from ★ to ★ 4 times more, making 5 lengths in total.

MAKING UP

Do **NOT** press. Stitch all 5 lengths together at centre.

DOLL

KIM HARGREAVES

YARN

Rowan Big Wool

A Tricky	030	2	x	100gm
B Smooch	031	1	x	100gm

or

Rowan Big Wool and Big Wool Tuft

A Wool Ice Blue	021	2	x	100gm
B Tuft Rugged	058	2	x	50gm

NEEDLES

1 pair 15mm (US 19) needles

TENSION

7½ sts and 9 rows to 10 cm measured over garter stitch using 15mm (US 19) needles.

FINISHED SIZE

Completed scarf measures 9 cm (3½ in) wide and 178 cm (70 in) long (excluding pompoms).

SCARF

Cast on 7 sts using 15mm (US 19) needles and yarn A.

Using yarn A, knit 2 rows.
Join in yarn B.
Using yarn B, knit 2 rows.
Rep last 4 rows until scarf measures 178 cm, ending with a WS row.
Using yarn A, cast off.

MAKING UP

PRESS as described on the information page.
Using yarn A, make two 10 cm diameter pompoms and attach one to each end of scarf.

PIA

KIM HARGREAVES

YARN

Two colour scarf

Rowan Biggy Print

A Tickle	237	2	x	100gm
B Fetish	236	3	x	100gm

Plain scarf

Rowan Big Wool Tuft

		5	x	50gm

(photographed in Frosty 055)

NEEDLES

1 pair 20mm (US 36) needles

TENSION

6½ sts and 7 rows to 10 cm measured over pattern using 20mm (US 36) needles.

FINISHED SIZE

Completed scarf measures 18 cm (7 in) wide. Excluding fringe, two colour scarf is 180 cm (71 in) long, and plain scarf is 220 cm (86½ in) long.

TWO COLOUR SCARF

Cast on 12 sts using 20mm (US 36) needles and yarn A.

Row 1 (RS): K1, ★yfwd, sl 1, K1, psso, rep from ★ to last st, K1.

Row 2: As row 1.

These 2 rows form patt.

Join in yarn B.

Using yarn B, patt 2 rows.

Using yarn A, patt 2 rows.

Rep last 4 rows until scarf measures 180 cm, ending with a WS row. Cast off.

PLAIN SCARF

Cast on 12 sts using 20mm (US 36) needles.

Row 1 (RS): K1, ★yfwd, sl 1, K1, psso, rep from ★ to last st, K1.

Rep this row until scarf measures 220 cm, ending with a WS row. Cast off.

MAKING UP

PRESS as described on the information page. Cut 30 cm lengths of yarn (for two colour scarf, use yarn B) and knot groups of 3 of these lengths through ends of scarf, making 5 knots evenly spaced across each end.

INFORMATION PAGE

TENSION

Obtaining the correct tension is perhaps the single factor which can make the difference between a successful garment and a disastrous one. It controls both the shape and size of an article, so **any** variation, can distort the finished look of the garment. We recommend that you knit a square in pattern and/or stocking stitch of perhaps 5 more stitches and rows than those given in the tension note. Press the finished square under a damp cloth and mark out the central 10cm square. If you have too many stitches to 10cm try again using thicker needles, if you have too few stitches to 10cm try again using finer needles.

SIZING AND SIZE DIAGRAM NOTE

The instructions are given for the smallest size. Where they vary, work the figures in brackets for the larger sizes. **One set of figures refers to all sizes.** Included with every pattern in this magazine is a '**size diagram**', the purpose of which is to enable you to accurately achieve a perfect fitting garment without the need for worry during knitting. The size diagram shows the finished width of the garment at the under-arm point, and it is this measurement that the knitter should choose first. Next look at the corresponding length for that size; if you are not happy with the total length which we recommend, adjust your own garment before beginning your armhole shaping - any adjustment after this point will mean that your sleeve will not fit into your garment easily - don't forget to take your adjustment into account if there is any side seam shaping. Finally, look at the sleeve length; the size diagram shows the finished sleeve measurement, taking into account

any top-arm insertion length. Measure your body between the centre of your neck and your wrist, this measurement should correspond to half the garment width plus the sleeve length. Again, your sleeve length may be adjusted, but remember to take into consideration your sleeve increases if you do adjust the length - you must increase more frequently than the pattern states to shorten your sleeve, less frequently to lengthen it.

KNITTING WITH COLOUR

There are two main methods of working colour into a knitted fabric: **Intarsia** and **Fairisle** techniques. The first method produces a single thickness of fabric and is usually used where a colour is only required in a particular area of a row and does not form a repeating pattern across the row, as in the fairisle technique.

Intarsia: The simplest way to do this is to cut short lengths of yarn for each motif or block of colour used in a row. Then joining in the various colours at the appropriate point on the row, link one colour to the next by twisting them around each other where they meet on the wrong side to avoid gaps. All ends can then either be darned along the colour join lines, as each motif is completed or then can be "knitted-in" to the fabric of the knitting as each colour is worked into the pattern. This is done in much the same way as "weaving-in" yarns when working the Fairisle technique and does save time darning-in ends. It is essential that the tension is noted for **Intarsia** as this may vary from the stocking stitch if both are used in the same pattern.

Fairisle type knitting: When two or three colours are worked repeatedly across a row, strand the yarn **not** in use loosely behind the stitches

being worked. If you are working with more than two colours, treat the "floating" yarns as if they were one yarn and always spread the stitches to their correct width to keep them elastic. It is advisable not to carry the stranded or "floating" yarns over more than three stitches at a time, but to weave them under and over the colour you are working. The "floating" yarns are therefore caught at the back of the work.

CROCHET TERMS

UK crochet terms and abbreviation have been used throughout. The list below gives the US equivalent where they vary.

Abbreviation	UK	US
dc	double crochet	single crochet
htr	half treble	half double crochet
tr	treble	double crochet
dtr	double treble	treble
ttr	triple treble	double treble
qtr	quadruple treble	triple treble

SLIP STITCH EDGINGS

When a row end edge forms the actual finished edge of a garment, you will often find a slip stitch edging is worked along this edge.

To work a slip stitch edging at the end of a RS row, work across the row until there is one st left on the left needle. Pick up the loop lying between the needles and place this loop on the right needle. Please note that this loop does NOT count as a st and is not included in any st counts. Now slip the last stitch knitwise with the yarn at the back (WS) of the work. At the beginning of the next row P together the first (slipped) stitch with the picked-up loop.

To work a slip stitch edging at the end of a WS row, work across the row until there is one st left on the left needle. Pick up the loop lying between the needles and place this loop on the right needle. Please note that this loop does NOT count as a st and is not included in any st counts. Now slip the last stitch purlwise with the yarn at the front (WS) of the work. At the beginning of the next row K together tbl the first (slipped) stitch with the picked-up loop.

FINISHING INSTRUCTIONS

After working for hours knitting a garment, it seems a great pity that many garments are spoiled because such little care is taken in the pressing and finishing process.

PRESSING

Darn in all ends neatly along the selvage edge or a colour join, as appropriate. Block out each piece of knitting using pins and gently press each piece, omitting the ribs, using a warm iron over a damp cloth. **Tip**: Take special care to press the edges, as this will make sewing up both easier and neater.

STITCHING

When stitching the pieces together, remember to match areas of colour and texture very carefully where they meet.

Use a seam stitch such as back stitch or mattress stitch for all main knitting seams, and join all ribs and neckband with a flat seam unless otherwise stated.

CONSTRUCTION

Having completed the pattern instructions, join left shoulder and neckband seams as detailed above.

Sew the top of the sleeve to the body of the garment using the method detailed in the pattern, referring to the appropriate guide:

Square set-in sleeves: Set sleeve head into armhole, the straight sides at top of sleeve to form a neat right-angle to cast-off sts at armhole on back and front.

Shallow set-in sleeves: Join cast-off sts at beg of armhole shaping to cast-off sts at start of sleeve-head shaping. Sew sleeve head into armhole, easing in shapings.

Set-in sleeves: Set in sleeve, easing sleeve head into armhole.

Join side and sleeve seams.

Slip stitch pocket edgings and linings into place. Sew on buttons to correspond with buttonholes. After sewing up, press seams and hems.

Ribbed welts and neckbands and any areas of garter stitch should not be pressed.

EXPERIENCE RATINGS

●   Easy, straight forward knitting

● ●   Suitable for the average knitter

ABBREVIATIONS

K	knit	**rev**	revers(e)(ing)	**sl1**	slip one stitch
P	purl	**rep**	repeat	**psso**	pass slipped stitch over
st(s)	stitch(es)	**alt**	alternate	**p2sso**	pass 2 slipped stitches over
inc	increas(e)(ing)	**cont**	continue	**tbl**	through back of loop
dec	decreas(e)(ing)	**patt**	pattern	**M1**	make one stitch by picking up
st st	stocking stitch (1 row K, 1 row P)	**tog**	together		horizontal loop before next stitch and
garter st	garter stitch (K every row)	**mm**	millimetres		knitting into back of it
beg	begin(ning)	**cm**	centimetres	**yfwd**	yarn forward
foll	following	**in(s)**	inch(es)	**yrn**	yarn round needle
rem	remain(ing)	**RS**	right side	**yon**	yarn over needle
		WS	wrong side	**cn**	cable needle

Stockist Information

AUSTRALIA
Australian Country Spinners
314 Albert Street,
Brunswick
Victoria 3056.
Tel: (03) 9380 3888

BELGIUM
Pavan
Meerlaanstraat 73
B9860 Balegem (Oosterzele)
Tel: (32) 9 221 8594

CANADA
Diamond Yarn
9697 St Laurent,
Montreal
Quebec H3L 2N1
Tel: (514) 388 6188
www.diamondyarns.com

Diamond Yarn (Toronto)
155 Martin Ross,
Unit 3
Toronto,
Ontario M3J 2L9
Tel: (416) 736 6111
www.diamondyarns.com

DENMARK
Individual stockists –
please contact Rowan for details

FRANCE
Elle Tricote
8 Rue du Coq
67000 Strasbourg
Tel: (33) 3 88 23 03 13
www.elletricote.com

GERMANY
Wolle & Design
Wolfshovener Strasse 76
52428 Julich-Stetternich
Tel: (49) 2461 54735
www.wolleundesign.de

HOLLAND
de Afstap
Oude Leliestraat 12
1015 AW Amsterdam
Tel: (31) 20 6231445

HONG KONG
East Unity Co Ltd
Unit B2, 7/F, Block B
Kailey Industrial Centre
12 Fung Yip Street
Chai Wan
Tel: (852) 2869 7110

ICELAND
Storkurinn
Laugavegi 59
Reykjavik
Tel: (354) 551 82 58

JAPAN
Puppy Co Ltd
TOC Building
7-22-17 Nishigotanda
Shinagwa-Ku
Tokyo
Tel: (81) 3 3494 2435

NEW ZEALAND
Individual stockists –
please contact Rowan for details

NORWAY
Pa Pinne
Tennisun 3D
0777 OSLO
Tel: (47) 909 62 818
www.paapinne.no

SWEDEN
Wincent
Norrtulsgaten 65
11345 Stockholm
Tel: (46) 8 673 70 60

U.S.A.
Rowan USA
4 Townsend West
Suite 8,
Nashua
New Hampshire 03063
Tel: (1 603) 886 5041/5043

For details of U.K. stockists or any other information
concerning this book please contact:

Rowan Yarns, Green Lane Mill, Holmfirth,
West Yorkshire HD9 2DX
Tel: +44 (0)1484 681881   Fax: +44 (0)1484 687920
Email: bigjustgotbigger@knitrowan.com www.knitrowan.com

Photographer Joey Toller • Stylist Kim Hargreaves • Hair & Make-up Annabel Hobbs • Models Alexa Chung, Elsa Plumley & James Eden
Reproduction in whole or any part of all material, including illustrations, in this publication is strictly forbidden unless prior consent of the publisher has
been given in writing. Yarn quantities are approximate as they are based on average requirements. Colour reproduction is as close as printing will allow.
Copyright Rowan 2004

BIG JUST GOT BIGGER